THE SOCIAL WORK EDUCATOR

THE SOCIAL WORK EDUCATOR
edited by JOSEPH SOFFEN

Readings on the Preparation and Induction
of Social Work Faculty

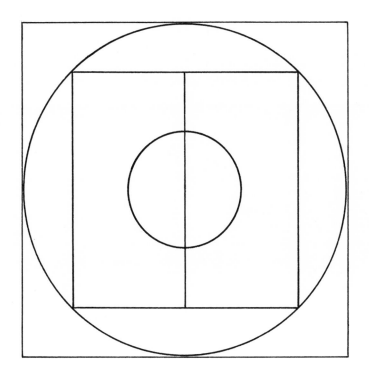

COUNCIL ON SOCIAL WORK EDUCATION
345 East 46th Street, New York, N.Y. 10017

Printed in the United States of America by
Sowers Printing Co., Lebanon, Pennsylvania, 1969

FOREWORD

Schools of social work have undergone major growth and change in recent years. The development of new graduate schools, the expansion of existing schools, the expansion of undergraduate programs in social welfare, and the introduction of curriculum innovations and new teaching media have brought increasing interest and concern with the preparation and induction of social work educators. Well-prepared faculty are needed in social work education at all levels.

Recognizing the importance of selecting and preparing social work educators for new and expanded roles, the Council on Social Work Education has given high priority to faculty development. *The Social Work Educator* represents one effort by CSWE to respond to the vital need for appropriate resources in the area of faculty development. This useful volume is a collection of papers written by social work educators with varied backgrounds and experience. It covers the areas of selection, preparation, and induction of social work educators.

Dr. Joseph Soffen, director of CSWE's faculty development project and author of the CSWE publication *Faculty Development in Professional Education*, served as compiler and editor of this volume. The Council wishes to extend sincere thanks to him for his efforts. Grateful acknowledgment is also extended to the eleven contributors to the publication. Thanks are also due to the National Institute of Mental Health, Health Services and Mental Health Administration, HEW, whose support made the publication of this volume possible.

The Council on Social Work Education takes pride in presenting *The Social Work Educator: Readings on the Preparation and Induction of Social Work Faculty.* It is our hope that this volume, along with Dr. Soffen's faculty development study and Richard Onken's *Survey of Faculty in Graduate Schools of Social Work*, will be of value to faculty, administrators, and students in graduate schools of social work, and undergraduate programs in social welfare, as well as to all those interested in or considering careers in social work education. A list of other CSWE publications related to faculty development appears on page 130.

Comments on this volume and suggestions for other publications needed are cordially invited.

ARNULF M. PINS

Executive Director

December, 1968

TABLE OF CONTENTS

FOREWORD v

INTRODUCTION ix

PART I   CHOOSING AND PREPARING FOR A CAREER IN
SOCIAL WORK EDUCATION

Choosing and Preparing for a Career in
Social Work Education 3

Selection and Preparation of Faculty for Schools of Social
Work   8
Eileen Blackey

The Attributes of a Social Work Educator 18
Ruth E. Smalley

Developing the Faculty: The Opportunities and Demands
of Teaching 25
Dame Eileen L. Younghusband

Four Components of Preparation for the Social Work
Educator   36
Joseph Soffen

To Learn to Teach: A Challenge to
Social Work Education. 53
Lila Swell

PART II   ON BECOMING A TEACHER: THE INDUCTION
PERIOD

On Becoming A Teacher: The Induction Period 65

Random Thoughts of a New Faculty Member 67
Anonymous

Orientation of New Faculty 69
Victoria Olds

On Becoming A Teacher 77
    Virginia L. Tannar

Practices and Problems in the Development of New Faculty:
  Introduction 84
    Ruth E. Smalley
  As Viewed by One School 86
    Rosa Wessel
  As Viewed by a New Faculty Member New to Full-
  Time Teaching 91
    Renee Berg
  As Viewed by A Faculty Member With Experience in
  Another School 95
    Joseph Soffen

PART III ". . . AND GLADLY TEACH"

". . . And Gladly Teach" 103

The Requirements and Rewards for Teaching 104
    Ruth E. Smalley

". . . And Gladly Teach" 110
    Helen Harris Perlman

BIBLIOGRAPHY 123

INTRODUCTION

There has been a continuing interest in the teacher as a pivotal concern in social work education over the years. Questions dealing with the personal qualities and professional qualifications needed by those who are responsible for preparing social workers for the challenge of changing and demanding professional practice have been proposed, pondered, and debated. Built upon the monumental contributions of the early educators for social work, such as Bertha Reynolds, Virginia Robinson, and Charlotte Towle, this area of interest has achieved more focus and precision in recent years. The present volume presents the more recent expression of this interest.

CONTINUING RECOGNITION OF NEED

In recent years there has been increasing interest in the teacher, throughout higher education in general, and in professional education more specifically. The efforts made by the social work sector of professional education for the improvement of teaching have contributed to other fields, and, in turn, have been enriched by them. In full recognition of this mutuality, an overview of the recent history within social work education will be useful.

Helping in the recruitment and selection of new faculty and assisting them to become educators in the best sense of the word has been one of the major "agenda items" of the Council on Social Work Education during the past 16 years. Faculty days and workshops on teaching at its Annual Program Meetings have been regularly scheduled. Emphasis on the teaching-learning process has been increasingly noted at these meetings. Beginning with the simple registry of unfilled faculty positions, the Council on Social Work Education has expanded its services to the active recruitment of more faculty members.

The direction of these activities has been fashioned by the Council on Social Work Education staff and committees. Within the past decade, contributions have come from several vantage points: the CSWE Committee on Advanced Education and, particularly, its Subcommittee on Preparation of Teachers; the CSWE Project on Field Instruction; and the CSWE Committee on Teaching Methodology and Materials.[1] A survey of

---

[1] These committee titles are now obsolete; in the restructuring of CSWE, their work is being continued within new divisions such as the Committee on Faculty and Teaching.

The Report of the Subcommittee on Preparation of Teachers will be found in Elizabeth G. Meier, "Preparation for Teaching Social Work," *Social Work Education Reporter,* Vol. 13, No. 3 (September, 1965), pp. 14 ff.

faculty of graduate schools of social work, completed in 1967, has given direction and impetus to recruitment and faculty development.[2] The CSWE publications in this area include: *The Teacher's Compendium; A Source Book of Readings on Teaching in Social Work; Annotated Bibliography on Audiovisual Instruction in Professional Education; The Social Work Education Reporter* (a quarterly) with a section on "Teaching News-Notes"; and the *Journal of Education for Social Work* (semi-annual). Both periodicals include items dealing with the improvement of teaching.

At the Annual Program Meeting in 1964, Dean Eileen Blackey of the School of Social Welfare, University of California, Los Angeles, identified the essence of the qualitative problem as follows:

> It seems incredible that we have done so little to train teachers for faculties of schools of social work. Our drive toward securing higher qualifications for practitioners has been constant. Our failure in settling for less than the best in the selection of teachers to prepare practitioners is an indictment which we must acknowledge and remove.[3]

Shortly thereafter, the CSWE Faculty Development Project undertook: (1) to clarify the sources of faculty personnel and the routes to positions in social work education, and (2) to develop proposals for sound and realistic patterns in the recruitment and pre-service preparation, induction, and continuing education of faculty. The report of the Faculty Development Project has been published by CSWE under the title *Faculty Development in Professional Education* (1968). Subsequently, a seven-year program has been undertaken to implement the recommendations of that project.

Faculty Development in Professional Education is addressed to the educational enterprise as a whole, and only incidentally to faculty. Its conclusions and recommendations are essentially at a policy level. The present volume, as one of the outcomes of the Faculty Development Project, is intended for several specific groups of readers. The selections will be read by deans and senior faculty with the goal of aiding them in their selection of new faculty or in their consultations with individuals who are exploring careers in social work education. They will be testing the formulations presented against their own criteria. On the other hand, those in the process of choosing, or at the point of undertaking this career, have their own perspective. They will match their personal qualities, enthusiasm, knowledge, skill, and expectations with suggestions, contained in the report, by recognized leaders in the field. Where they find congruence, they will be

---

[2] Richard Onken, *A Survey of Faculty in Graduate Schools of Social Work* (New York: Council on Social Work Education, 1968).

[3] Eileen Blackey, "Issues in Social Work Education—New and Changing Demands Made of the Profession," *Education For Social Work: Proceedings of the Twelfth Annual Program Meeting* (New York: Council on Social Work Education, 1964), p. 86.

reassured and stimulated; where they do not, they will seek clarification and proceed with more direction in their planning. It is also contemplated that this collection may be useful as a point of departure for individual study by new faculty, or in classes and seminars for new teachers. Individuals working on their doctorates may also be influenced by this publication to choose careers in the area of education.

In his work on the project, the editor of this volume became more firmly convinced of the usefulness of separating the three stages of faculty development earlier identified by Blackey. These include: (1) acquisition of knowledge and experience basic to responsible entry into teaching; (2) sound development in the initial stages of teaching; and (3) continuing education and development toward higher levels of achievement.[4]

Part I includes selections which are pertinent to the pre-service phase, and Part II selections pertinent to the induction phase. The continuing education phase is neglected not because it is less important—its importance is surely evident—but rather because material of an equal order is not as readily available. It would seem advisable, at any rate, that a separate volume on continuing education eventually be prepared for its own audience. Similarly, no attempt is made to select from the vast literature on "methodology" as such, for obvious reasons. The bibliography, however, while hardly exhaustive, suggests some avenues for further investigation for which the selections may serve as starting points.

---

[4] Eileen Blackey, "Selection and Preparation of Faculty for Schools of Social Work," reprinted in the present volume, p. 8.

Part I

Choosing and Preparing for a Career in Social Work Education

CHOOSING AND PREPARING FOR A CAREER IN SOCIAL WORK EDUCATION

Social work education may be considered as including undergraduate, master's, and advanced education, as well as the whole range of non-degree offerings, under the institutional auspices of college or university. In addition, of course, social agencies conduct their own in-service programs.

In the 1965-66 academic year, there were 5,638 faculty in graduate schools of social work. Of these, 826 had either full-time classroom or administrative responsibilities, or combinations of these two; there were 407 full-time field instructors. In addition, there were 690 part-time classroom instructors and 3,715 part-time field instructors.[1] These numbers show a 100 percent increase in full-time faculty between 1955 and 1966, while the number of part-time faculty increased almost 60 percent. Because of the diversity and complexity of arrangements and the deployment of graduate school faculty who teach in undergraduate or post-master's programs, data are not available at this time to provide a total picture.

Of those who have classroom teaching responsibilities, 60 percent teach in more than one curricular area; two-thirds in the methods sequences, and 30 percent in the human growth and social environment sequence. Twenty-five percent teach social welfare policy courses, 20 percent teach research and serve as advisors for student research projects, and nine percent teach administration courses.

Routes and Points of Entry

Current faculty have come to their positions by way of three major routes, within each of which there are different points of entry. The traditional and most frequent route, the *professional* route, has been movement to a school-based position following a period of practice. However, within this route there are several points of entry, e.g., after a few years in practice, after receiving the MSW, or a late-in-career shift. Some come by way of the part-time point of entry. Many begin to teach without having any advanced education. Thirty percent of current faculty have studied in programs of advanced education, but have not earned doctorates. About ten percent of all faculty have doctoral degrees, but less than one percent of field instructors

[1] Richard Onken, *Survey of Faculty in Graduate Schools of Social Work* (New York: Council on Social Work Education, 1968).

have doctorates. Fifteen percent of new faculty in 1963-64 had doctorates or earned them within two years after beginning teaching.

A second route follows the *academic* pattern, in which work on the doctorate is undertaken with a minimum of social work practice experience. For example, of 18 recently appointed faculty who received their doctorates in 1963 or 1964, more than half had less than four years of practice experience.

The third route may be conceived as the *acculturation* route, by which the non-social workers (currently about 11 percent) whose major education has been in a related field become "acculturated" to social work and social work education after becoming faculty members in a school of social work.

Obviously, each of these groupings and subgroupings, depending upon the point of entry and the route used, demonstrate different strengths and qualities of experience. Together they represent a heterogeneous collectivity which offers richness of knowledge and experience to the educational scene. They also represent a variety of differential needs or gaps in readiness for assuming major educational responsibilities. To these we shall return in Part II.

THE SCHOOL WITHIN THE UNIVERSITY

As schools of social work have become integral parts of their universities, they have been confronted by the need to reconcile their minority culture, derived from agency life, with that of the university. In addition, general issues in higher education, which have remained unresolved for almost a century, have become issues for social work education.

Social work education has had to struggle for recognition within the status hierarchy of the university and of the professional schools. As recently as 1963, social work was identified (invidiously, it seems to us) as an "emerging or marginal profession." Some have noted that the sociology of social workers contrasts with that of academicians and with faculty in other branches of professional education. Whether there are in fact caste or class differences is immaterial; some perceive them and more feel them.

Contrasting educational orientations between the academic and the professional have been noted. For example, the academic goal orientation is characterized by "to know" and the professional orientation is characterized by "to do;" the academic value orientation is to "truth," the professional is to "service."

The question of *career line* arises more sharply in the professional school than in the academic disciplines. The typical career line for the academic professor is relatively simple to describe; he pursues graduate study and moves more or less directly into teaching. This is also true, to some extent, for some positions in other professional schools.

With the growing recognition that the career line for the social work

4

educator is a distinctive and substantive one—a scholarly one within a community of scholars—we find ourselves in the midst of extremely complex and unresolved issues.

The Doctorate

The doctoral degree has always been the symbol for the achievement of the qualities of scholarliness. But while the symbol has remained constant during the last century, what it signifies has been questioned. It has become the "glory, jest and riddle of the world of higher learning in America."[2] The symbolic meaning of the degree has been vigorously debated for some time now. There are those who argue that the doctorate is the *sine qua non* for scholarly qualification and for full faculty citizenship. They defend it with conviction about its time-tested values. Wilson asserts that:

> The degree is right because it joins the concept of present knowing and future learning. In spite of all complaints about the dissertation, the idea is important to good teaching. A teacher who is not probing the unknown may unconsciously convey the impression that knowledge is static—something to be memorized.[3]

Others, with a figurative shrug of the shoulders, agree that though the doctorate may not insure all that is claimed for it, no better alternative is available. Some cynically refer to it as the "immutable Ph.D.," unresponsive to needed reforms. It has been challenged as preparation for inappropriate ends, or simply as unnecessary. It has also been called an "American fetish."

From every vantage point come suggestions for reform. Some would change the boundaries of advanced study by upgrading the master's or downgrading the doctorate. Others take the present boundaries as given and suggest modifications within the established boundaries to strengthen the degrees, such as modifying the dissertation requirement, the language requirement, or the sequence and timing of the requirements.

The debate has persisted for more than half a century in this country, and the literature of that debate is copious. Berelson summarizes:

> It is instructive and often entertaining to review the discussions of the AAU (Association of American Universities) in the first few years of its existence. . . . There is hardly a topic active today that has not been debated then, and not infrequently in the same terms. Fellowships, the meaning of research, the character of the dissertation, the quality of the students, the foreign language requirement, the major-minor problem at the doctoral

---

[2] Moody E. Prior, "The Doctor of Philosophy Degree," in *Graduate Education Today,* Everett Walters, ed. (Washington: American Council on Education, 1965), p. 30.

[3] O. Meredith Wilson, "The Ph.D. Program as Preparation for Teaching," *Association of American Colleges Bulletin,* Vol. 44, No. 1 (March, 1958), pp. 55-59. See also R. J. Henle, S.J., "The Soundness of the American Ph.D. Programs," in *Improving College Teaching,* Calvin B. T. Lee, ed. (Washington: American Council on Education, 1967).

level, the proper examinations, the role of the Master's, preparation for college teaching . . . all these topics come up in the first years of the AAU.[4]

Teaching in the University

The basic problem, it appears, is the status of teaching qua teaching within the university, although the debate is most frequently joined as though the issues were teaching *versus* research, one flourishing only at the expense of the other. That research activities are more easily discerned and more readily rewarded is frequently noted. But the source of uneasiness lies in the fact that doctoral programs are not planned to prepare potential faculty members specifically for the teaching they will do. The President's Commission on Higher Education in 1947 concluded that:

> College teaching is the only major learned profession for which there does not exist a well-defined program of preparation directed toward developing the skills which it is essential for the practitioner to possess.[5]

What constitutes readiness for teaching and how doctoral study prepares for it are at once obscure and loaded questions. While few minimize the importance of good teaching, current thinking in the academic community with respect to teaching methodology is, to understate the case, without consensus. Some remain unconvinced that there is, in fact, an art of teaching. They are suspicious of the "educationist" and fear that attention to teaching methodology will threaten standards of subject matter excellence. Others believe that there may be an art, but are not sure about what it is or, at any rate, that it can be acquired. The art is charismatic and not transmissible; "good teachers are born, not made," they claim. A third group holds vigorously that ability to teach can be acquired and transmitted, and insists eloquently on the urgency of providing experiences for the improvement of university teaching. The problem is further complicated by the fact that some fear that administrative involvement in the *how* of teaching may become, or be construed, as a threat to academic freedom because the *what* is too easily contaminated by the *how*. They would be willing to consider attention to the teaching component in pre-service education, but not as part of an in-service program.

THE SCHOOL AND THE PROFESSION

In addition to the quantitative pressures from the field, there are qualitative imperatives for the kind of faculty needed, which must not be overlooked.

---

[4] Bernard Berelson, *Graduate Education in the United States* (New York: McGraw-Hill, 1960), p. 17.

[5] *Higher Education for American Democracy, A Report of the President's Commission on Higher Education*, Vol. 4, *Staffing Higher Education* (New York: Harper and Bros., 1947), p. 16.

The nature of professional education is such that it must be responsive to changing needs from the "front lines" and, at the same time, give impetus to changing the field itself. Professional education must be both reactive and initiative. A qualitatively different kind of practice is now expected even in the most traditional settings. We are witnessing redefinition of the scope and function of social work. The development of new programs in new settings under new sponsorship creates its own special demands. John Gardner, when he was Secretary of the United States Department of Health, Education, and Welfare, predicted that many of the agencies in the next generation "will bear little resemblance to the agencies of today."[6]

Changing practice requires new knowledge and new formulations of what is known and what is about to be known. Research was described in the Hollis-Taylor Report[7] in 1951 as a "long-known shortcoming" of the social work profession. Despite some progress, this shortcoming has not been eliminated and provides an imperative *from the field* to the school of social work even stronger than any expectation from the university for research leadership by faculty. There are also deep implications for effectiveness of research teaching, and, even more pervasively, for research-mindedness on the part of the whole faculty.

The five selections which follow deal with the issues which have been touched upon so briefly here. They are essentially in agreement, yet each author, in partializing the overall question, develops and gives expression to his answers with differing perspectives. All posit the case for "planned faculty development upon the assumption that both teaching and curriculum planning are complex activities for which systematic learning and practice are needed." Dean Blackey has provided the base for viewing the development of faculty as a continuing one, with distinctive inputs necessary at each stage. (This base has served as a rationale for the organization of the present volume.) Dean Smalley casts the elements of preparation as "attributes." Although Dame Younghusband speaks from an international vantage point, her vision of a fruitful educational institution as "a society in which students and teachers are both learning together" is pertinent to those concerned with social work education on this continent. Dr. Soffen builds upon the first three selections and specifies "components" of preparation. Dr. Swell provides an approach to operationalizing a program for social work classroom teachers.

---

[6] John W. Gardner, "Remarks," *Journal of Education for Social Work*, Vol. 2, No. 1 (Spring, 1966), p. 7.

[7] Ernest W. Hollis and Alice Taylor, *Social Work Education in the United States* (New York: Columbia University Press, 1951).

SELECTION AND PREPARATION OF FACULTY FOR SCHOOLS OF SOCIAL WORK

by Eileen Blackey *

(In this article, Dean Blackey has reformulated "transition to teaching," the phrase used in earlier years, to urge a continuing process for the improvement of teaching. She identifies three stages in that process and outlines their distinctive qualities. Ed.)

THE OVERVIEW

Although there will be—as there should be—differences of opinion as to how we may best attack and resolve the problems of preparation of faculty for schools of social work, the urgency of the need for new approaches and solutions can no longer be questioned. It is both comforting and disconcerting to find ourselves swept up in a veritable tidal wave of concern with issues in education at all levels in our society. We cannot consider our problems in social work education without reference to this national upsurge, which is a reflection not of parochial interests, but of a wide and deep concern with all our educational institutions as instruments of social change and humanitarian advancement.

The teaching profession in the United States seems to have developed a peculiar set of mores over the years. Traditionally, teachers at the elementary and secondary school level have been required to undergo formal training in teaching methods as well as subject-matter, in institutions developed for the purpose, such as normal schools, teachers' colleges, and undergraduate departments of education. Yet, until very recently, little or no formal preparation for teaching has been required of educators at the undergraduate level and beyond, and development of such preparation seems practically non-existent. The higher one goes in the academic hierarchy, the less the importance attached to formal teacher training.

Why is this? Do we think that once students reach university level they

---

* Originally published in Journal of Education for Social Work, Vol. 1, No. 1 (Spring, 1965), pp. 5-12. Dr. Blackey is currently a consultant for the Council on Social Work Education; she was formerly dean of the School of Social Welfare, University of California in Los Angeles.

must assume the entire responsibility for their own education? Do we assume that mastery of a particular field of knowledge, be it botany or casework, automatically prepares us to transmit it to students? Is it an implicit assumption of the American academic culture that higher education bestows on its anointed the mantle of excellence just by virtue of their having joined its ranks? Have we lent an aura of prestige to faculty status which makes "learning how to teach" seem beneath the dignity of someone so appointed? And have our universities and colleges permitted the frantic pursuit of research to eclipse our responsibility to put the fruits of research to use through skillful and creative teaching?

While these questions apply to all institutions of higher education, this article will focus on the selection and preparation of classroom faculty within the context of the requirements and expectations of social work education. Many of the ideas presented will be as applicable to field instructors as to classroom teachers, but there is so much which is unique about a plan for school-based field instructors that the subject is deserving of fuller treatment in another article.

WHAT ARE WE LOOKING FOR IN OUR SELECTION OF FACULTY?

Aside from the practical problem of matching the qualifications of a particular candidate to a particular post, the selection of individual faculty members and the building of a faculty as an orchestrated whole is a very complex process. The desirable personal attributes or qualities of candidates, together with their educational and professional qualifications as educators, are the paramount factors in this selection process.

Personal Attributes

Two working papers presented at the Thirteenth Annual Program Meeting of the Council on Social Work Education in Denver have a direct bearing on the first of these considerations. In her discussion of "The Attributes of a Social Work Educator," Ruth Smalley pleads for "an 'interesting' self in lively possession of its own uniqueness as an individual."[1] She stresses the need for teachers who are "vigorous, interesting people . . . motivated and able to use their individual selves within the discipline of social work education, toward accomplishing the purposes of social work education, through appropriate but varied teaching methods";[2] people with scholarly qualities of intellectual curi-

---

[1] Ruth E. Smalley, "The Attributes of a Social Work Educator." Reprinted in the present volume, pp. 18-24.

[2] *Ibid.*

9

osity and discipline, a clear commitment to teaching, and interest, motivation, and capacity for continuing the development of themselves as teachers.[3]

Maurice Connery, in "Becoming a Social Work Educator," speaks of "identity" as an attribute, stressing that a successful social work educator must first achieve and maintain his identity as a social worker. Noting that identity determines in a critical way what we perceive, as well as the patterns within which we organize our perceptions, Connery points up the necessity of determining in what ways the perceptive set of the social work educator is similar to, as well as different from, that of the social work practitioner: "Just as there are individuals on school of social work staffs who are social workers and not educators, so too are there social work educators who deny or ignore their social work identity or that the business we are about is *social work education*."[4]

The elusive and rare quality of "excellence" which social work, in common with the other professions, seeks in its educators is perhaps easier to recognize than to analyze and describe. In speaking of excellence in college teaching, Earl Pullias suggests that among the prerequisite qualities are imagination and independence of mind, respect for the essential integrity of all human beings, commitment to well-defined personal values, and a sense of identity. He emphasizes the importance of knowing something of who and what one is, and where one is going, if one is to help students find themselves and their directions.[5] John Gardner, in his book on excellence, reminds us that excellence occurs in many forms, but all forms of excellence are founded on two principles: an appreciation of the plurality of values in our pluralistic society, and a universally recognized, honored philosophy of individual fulfillment.[6]

Also relevant to educational excellence is the concept of the teacher as an artist, and of education as a medium of creative self-expression. Robert Henri, an American painter of the 1920's, saw art as the province of every human being regardless of his medium: "When the artist is alive in any person, whatever his kind of work may be, he becomes an inventive, searching, daring, self-expressing creature."[7] The artist is alive in the truly excellent teacher.

---

[3] *Ibid.*

[4] Maurice F. Connery, "Becoming a Social Work Educator," paper given at the Council on Social Work Education, Thirteenth Annual Program Meeting, Denver, January, 1965.

[5] Earl V. Pullias, *Toward Excellence in College Teaching* (Dubuque, Iowa: W. C. Brown Co., 1963).

[6] John W. Gardner, *Excellence: Can We be Equal and Excellent Too?* (New York: Harper & Row, 1961).

[7] Robert Henri, *The Art Spirit* (Philadelphia: J. B. Lippincott Co., 1930).

The constellation of personal attributes and qualities essential to the realization of excellence in education cannot be demanded of everyone; necessarily, many teachers will be employed who lack some of these attributes. On the other hand, many individuals have latent qualities which can be nurtured and developed. The development of a first-rate teacher is a gradual process of personal growth, and our assessment at the point of recruitment of an individual's personal attributes and potential for change may be quite different from our assessment of him a few years later.

Educational and Professional Qualifications

It is apparent that in order to discuss educational and professional qualifications, one must determine the tasks and purposes for which the social work teacher is expected to be qualified. Should he be qualified to prepare candidates for the master's degree to enter professional practice? To meet his commitment as a faculty member to the promotion of the educational aims of his school? To make a contribution to human affairs indirectly, through his influence on his students, and directly, through his own original research and thought? Yes, all of these responsibilities seem to be implicit in the teacher's role. If this is so, one problem that confronts us is determination of the educational and experience base for meeting these various responsibilities.

The assumption in most academic circles is that acquisition of the doctoral degree is the logical route to university teaching. Social work education seems to be moving in this direction but is caught in the same dilemma which confronts social work practice: there is an overwhelming demand for a small supply of candidates. Until some redress of this imbalance can be accomplished, any consideration of teacher recruitment must be concerned with candidates who have only the master's degree, as well as those who have the doctorate.

This premise leads us logically to an examination of what we look for in our educators and the extent to which each of these educational routes meets our requirements. For example, is successful experience as a practitioner essential to teaching, and is this true for all parts of the curriculum? The answer to this question might establish successful social work practice as a prerequisite to teaching, perhaps not in all courses, but certainly in the methods courses. The substance, range, diversity, and duration of such practice could also be considered.[8]

Is it necessary that all teachers be researchers actively engaged in doing research, or can effective teaching also be achieved by individuals with a sound research orientation and appreciation of its uses in teaching? The research prerequisite needs clarification. While it may be advisable for doctoral candidates to conduct research, it may be sufficient for potential teachers

---

[8] Smalley, *op. cit.*

11

in other teacher-training programs to learn to utilize as "consumers" research conducted by others.

And, finally, how do we define the requirements for commitment to education in the larger sense? An answer to this question requires the development of a core curriculum in social work education which can form the requisite foundation for educational commitment.

Basic to any of these prerequisites is the requirement of knowledge, in range and depth, of one's own field and of fields sufficiently related to it to influence changes in theory and practice. The criteria for judging and measuring this qualification in a prospective candidate are still inadequately developed.

If we apply to the problem of preparation for social work education the same educational principles which we apply to preparation for practice, we can identify three major stages of learning: (1) acquisition of knowledge and experience basic to responsible entry into teaching; (2) sound development in the initial stages of teaching; and (3) continuing education and development toward higher levels of achievement.

THE FIRST STAGE

The basic "core content" of the first stage of preparation for responsible entrance into social work education concerns the nature of learning and the transmission of knowledge. This core content cannot be learned as part of an apprenticeship after appointment to a faculty. We have not yet sufficiently identified and formulated this "core," but it must certainly include familiarity with current learning theory and a working competence with the concept Bruner calls "structure" of a subject—a grasp of the underlying structure or significance of complex knowledge, even to the degree that learning properly under optimum conditions enables one to "learn how to learn."[9] Our own valiant efforts toward conceptualization and generalization of knowledge and experience in our field as a basis for facilitating the transfer of learning, though indicating progress in this area, still do not provide learning designated to produce general understanding of the structure of a subject matter at the level indicated by Bruner. This is of course due in part to the stage of development of our knowledge and theory, but we have an opportunity for experimentation in how to teach fundamental structure effectively and how to provide learning conditions that foster it; how to develop curricula as an effective vehicle for this important task; how to know more about learners generally and our own in particular; how to acquire knowledge and skills essential for working with groups of learners with the goal of helping

---

[9] Jerome S. Bruner, *The Process of Education* (Cambridge: Harvard University Press, 1960).

each student to achieve his optimum intellectual and professional development; how to become familiar with the resources for teaching and how to select the media and methodologies most appropriate to one's goals.

In other words, entrance into social work education today implies entrance into a total educational complex and the responsibilities that reside in it. The knowledge and competence required to fulfill these responsibilities cannot be assumed to have been acquired in practice, no matter how extensive or at what level. They must then be provided either in doctoral programs or through other programs designed for master's degree candidates whose primary career goal is teaching rather than practice.

Doctoral Programs as a Route

Despite the still small number of those holding doctoral degrees, it is true that a substantial number of those who enter doctoral programs do so with a career goal of joining faculties of schools of social work. Why not, therefore, make education a specific area of specialization in the doctoral program? Many of our doubts about making preparation for teaching part of the doctoral program are based on fear of "diluting" the scholarly integrity of the doctoral program. Or we assume that completing a doctoral program automatically prepares one to join a faculty, and draw the equally fallacious conclusion that our doctoral programs already educate for teaching and research.

Actually, with the introduction of social work education as a specific area of specialization, research within the specialization could be focused on the design, testing, and evaluation of approaches to learning theory, curricula development, and teaching methods. One reason for our limited advances in social work education as a field is our lack of research into these processes, which currently receive attention in our doctoral programs to a negligible extent, if at all.

The core course content identified earlier as essential preparation for social work education could be included as elective seminars without jeopardy to the core curriculum of the doctoral program. While experts from other professions may be called upon to assist us in this task, the development and teaching of this core curriculum in social work education must, of course, be carried out by social work educators.

A difficult issue to resolve is the place of practice teaching in the doctoral program. If we assume that the first year of actual teaching will be a closely supervised, well-integrated continuation of the "learning to teach" process, it does not seem necessary to divert a very large share of the doctoral students' time into practice teaching. On the other hand, involvement in a research project concerned with some aspect of social work education will in itself necessitate observation of and active participation in important processes —for example, working on faculty committees concerned with curriculum development, serving as a teaching assistant, or becoming a career teacher within a more structured program of teacher training. Acquiring an educational stance or readiness for engagement in social work education would be the goal of the doctoral program, rather than the molding of a full-fledged teacher. In fact, the process of emerging as a teacher can be much more effectively achieved within the particular educational climate of the schools with which the new teacher is associated.

The Master's Degree Route

What of the preparation of teachers who do not enter social work education by way of doctoral programs? This is a greater problem, both in terms of volume (at least as of now) and in relation to how best to develop a program of study. Certainly, if the principle of preparation for entry into social work education is valid, prospective faculty members recruited directly from the field of practice should also be given the opportunity to, and be required to, complete a study program which would prepare them for their educational responsibilities. The educational task in planning such a program is even more complex. For example, it can be assumed that a student in a doctoral program will be introduced to new and developing areas of knowledge both within our own field and allied fields, including research findings and their impact on educational content. Learning to become a social work educator in this climate is quite different from having to make the leap from "doing" into "teaching" in one giant step.

What are the possibilities for teacher preparation of prospective faculty members in this latter group? It would appear that there are two. First, it might be feasible to develop a career program for teachers which would require one or two years of study for completion, but would lead to certification as a social work educator rather than to a doctoral degree. However, such programs should be initiated only at schools which offer a doctoral program, with opportunities to participate in doctoral program courses and to be exposed to the educational climate of advanced study. Such a proposal raises all the usual questions of what academic recognition a certification program should receive and whether, in comparison with doctoral study, it would attract candidates. However, until all schools of social work can realistically require the doctoral degree as a basis for faculty appointment, and all the available positions can be filled by doctoral degree holders, it seems likely that schools of social work seeking faculty would be eager to hire teachers from a well-developed certification program. A program of this duration would make possible a broader curriculum encompassing new fields of knowledge and placing greater emphasis on research developments and their use.

The second possibility for this category of prospective faculty members would be a shorter-term educational program, preferably a full-time summer program, where a curriculum embodying the core content of social

14

work education could be taught. Elective courses should be included which up-date social work knowledge and present material from other fields, such as social science theory, relevant to the areas in which individuals are planning to teach. Such a program should become prerequisite for faculty appointment, supported by fellowships or salary. For example, university appointments usually begin with the fiscal year, July 1, but academic responsibilities do not begin until the opening of the academic year in September. If a school recruits a candidate who is promising in every other respect, what is to prevent the school from making his appointment contingent on attendance at a summer program designed to help him become a social work educator? Since the individual would already be receiving salary, the only other expenses for which the school would be responsible would be transportation, living expenses, and tuition. Funds to cover these expenses could certainly be sought from outside funding sources.

It is apparent that not every school of social work can operate its own summer program for new faculty. Rather, those schools with the best resources for conducting them should establish regional educational centers, and other schools utilizing them for teacher training should contribute enough financially, through adequate tuition fellowships, to guarantee a high order of faculty and program. As experience is gained with such a plan at the beginning level, development of advanced programs as a part of continuing education for faculty members would be an essential extension of these opportunities.

To be of maximum value, the summer session should be followed by a first-year experience as a faculty member planned in much the same way as that described below for a faculty member recruited directly from a doctoral program.

SECOND AND THIRD STAGES OF LEARNING

Responsibility for the second and third stages of professional development must rest with the school to which the individual is appointed. Here it is important to recognize that there are certain elements of education for teaching which must be acquired *before* employment, others which can only be introduced *after* a person becomes a faculty member, and still others for which only the individual *himself* can be responsible, as in the development of artistry in teaching, self-development through keeping abreast and ahead of knowledge in his own field and areas related to it, and engagement in scholarly pursuits through research and writing.

A school's responsibility to its new faculty members is many-sided. The school must orient the new faculty member to the school's program, to the university community and the social work community of which the school is a part, and to his particular teaching assignments and work load. The school can most effectively meet these responsibilities through a tutorial plan which enables the new teacher to be associated in a learning role with a senior colleague, in his field where possible. Such a tutorial plan should provide opportunities for the new faculty member to "sit in" on courses taught by others on the faculty in order to get a sense of the curriculum as a whole, to plan and teach his own courses in close consultation with his tutorial advisor, and to participate in committee work on curriculum development and other aspects of the educational program. However, the new recruit must be allowed sufficient time to absorb and integrate what he is learning.

Each tutorial plan must be specifically adapted to the new faculty member's background and experience, as well as to his particular assignment. While his relationship to his tutorial advisor should be primary, opportunities should be provided for him to consult any other experienced faculty members who can be instrumental in his development. His own learning about teaching should be a planned, systematic experience in which recordings or notes on his teaching sessions are used for discussion in regularly scheduled conferences with his tutorial advisor. Every effort should be made to bring out the unique talents and creativity of the new teacher and to encourage his experimentation in style and methodology. Introduction to the wealth of resources available to teachers, and help in their selection and utilization, should be part of the learning process.

Opportunities for the ongoing development of faculty should be made available both within the school and outside. Faculty seminars and colloquia, individual guidance directed toward the refinement and enhancement of knowledge and excellence in teaching and education, and opportunities for innovation and experimentation in education, should be built into a school's environment.

An essential instrument of the continuing progress of faculty is the development of evaluative criteria by which faculty members can measure their own advancement and by which the school can identify areas in which the performance of a faculty member can be strengthened. Development of such criteria is in itself an enriching experience for faculty.

Resources outside the school are increasingly becoming available. Workshops and institutes—for example, the highly praised summer workshop on undergraduate curriculum development in "social welfare as a social institution" held at Michigan State University in 1964—provide both theoretical and laboratory learning for the participants.

It should also be mentioned that we do not exploit sufficiently the opportunities deriving from what other schools are doing, through exchange of faculty, joint working conferences of faculties on particular issues or subjects, regional workshops for new faculty which pool the resources of several schools, even joint study-travel projects. The California Teachers Associa-

16

tion sponsors a "Teacher-to-Teacher" program, organized for the purpose of providing classroom teachers with an opportunity to have first-hand contact with school systems and teachers in other lands and cultures. A domestic version of such a program might be an interesting venture in educational communication.

How does one bring a subject as intriguing and challenging as this to a close, particularly when so much is left unexplored? Perhaps it can best be done by referring again to the postulates on which this article is based.

Formal preparation for undertaking the tasks of social work education, of which teaching is a core component, is a responsibility of the profession which must be given priority. Infinitely more exploration and study of what the obligations and processes of social work education are must be undertaken as a basis for determining of what such preparation should consist. The difficult task confronts us of determining in what ways and through what types of programs we can best develop our teacher training, but experimentation must begin. Our inquiries must be conducted and our solutions pursued within the larger context of higher education in general. And, always, our activities should be conceived of as opportunities to contribute to what John W. Gardner describes as the "ever-renewing society . . . within which continuous innovation, rebirth, and renewal are fostered."[10]

---

[10] John W. Gardner, "Renewal of the Universities," paper delivered at the Council of Presidents, Association of State Universities and Land Grant Colleges, Chicago, November, 1963.

THE ATTRIBUTES OF A SOCIAL WORK EDUCATOR

by Ruth E. Smalley *

"Teaching is not a lost art but the regard for it is a lost tradition," writes Jacques Barzun in *Teacher in America*.[1] This sparkling and iconoclastic book takes spirited issue with the use of the words "educator" and "education," preferring "teacher" and "teaching" as simpler and more accurate. "Education," Barzun points out, "comes from within; it is a man's own doing, or rather it happens to him—sometimes because of the teaching he has had, sometimes in spite of it."[2] ". . . The business of the . . . teacher is not education but teaching."[3]

So, to rephrase our topic as a question, "What are we looking for in social work teachers?"

But first, let us divide social work teachers into class teachers and field teachers and establish some mutual attributes and some attributes unique, in degree at least, to each.

A third try, then, at a title for the first part of this paper yields "Some Desirable Attributes and Qualifications for Class Teachers in Graduate Schools of Social Work." Let us begin with "Class Teachers in Graduate Schools" and come to "of Social Work" later.

ATTRIBUTES OF CLASS TEACHERS

An "Interesting" Self in Lively Possession of Its Own Uniqueness as an Individual

Any studied attempt to produce "professional selves" is in danger of turning out dull uniformity, faceless anonymity, "castes" of doctors, lawyers, social

---

[1] Jacques Barzun, *Teacher in America* ("Doubleday Anchor Books" [Garden City, N. Y.: Doubleday & Company, Inc., 1954]), p. 16.

[2] *Ibid.*, p. 10.

[3] *Ibid.*, pp. 9, 10.

---

* This position statement was the basis of a discussion at a workshop session at the CSWE Thirteenth Annual Program Meeting, January 21, 1965, Denver, Colorado. Dr. Smalley retired as Dean of the University of Pennsylvania School of Social Work in 1966. After her retirement, she served for one year as acting director of Educational Services of CSWE, and worked on several international projects.

workers, teachers, or whatever. A teacher who is primarily a "professional self" tends to produce students who are primarily "professional selves." Ideally, schools of social work should admit and develop vigorous, interesting men and women who can use their whole, rich selves within the discipline of a profession and through the profession's methods, to accomplish the profession's purposes. Such schools demand social work teachers who are themselves vigorous, interesting people, who contribute to a single faculty a range and scope of different kinds of people, motivated and able to use their individual selves within the discipline of social work education to accomplish the purposes of social work education through appropriate and varied teaching methods. A faculty composed of such teachers makes any school vastly richer in its gestalt than one whose recruitment effort has been devoted to finding persons who fit a rigid prescription for an "ideal teacher."

Scholarly Qualities

Scholarly qualities are based on an interest in the life of the mind and the pursuit of such a life by choice, because it is congenial. This basic interest includes intellectual curiosity and the motivation and discipline to add continuously to one's general knowledge as well as to one's knowledge of his particular area of concentration, and to contribute to development and communication of knowledge through research and publication.

This particular attribute is both tested and developed through doctoral study, but doctoral study neither insures it nor is always essential to it.

Teaching Skill and Commitment

Not all scholars are good teachers, and good teachers vary in the character and degree of their scholarship. But, having established an intellectual and scholarly attitude as essential to all teachers at the graduate level, we must not forget that interest in, commitment to, and *skill* in teaching constitute a different and equally necessary attribute. Many a creative artist finds teaching a bore and a frustration. He wants to express his dream, his passion, his vision as he sees and feels it; what "the other" does with it is of neither interest nor concern to him. But a good teacher has to care, not only about *what* he teaches, but about *whom* he teaches and *how* he teaches. This calls for an interest in fostering and nurturing the growth and development of the lives he influences, finding his own fulfillment in theirs. It calls, furthermore, for the development of teaching skill, which can be learned. Much has been developed recently in learning theory and teaching theory. How shall a social work teacher acquire that knowledge and develop teaching skill? Certainly, greater application of learning theory is badly needed in curriculum building and in school administration, as well as in actual teaching. For one thing, such theory establishes the distinction between the logic of knowledge and the logic of learning, a distinction which has important ramifications in the field agency as well as in the classroom.

But how shall teacher preparation be developed so as to assure the most effective and richly contributive faculty possible for graduate schools of social work? What is the best setting for the formal preparation of the social work teacher as teacher, and how shall it be made available? As an advanced program wholly within a school of education? The wide variation in such schools and their emphasis on preparation for primary- and secondary-level education, as well as recent criticisms of their curricula, raise doubts about this alternative. As a concentration within a doctoral program in a school of social work, with certain units of study drawn from education or other graduate divisions? This raises questions about the nature of the academic program and the supervised "field work in teaching" which would constitute the concentration, and how the concentration would be related to the total program of doctoral study.

As a planned in-service training program for teaching for which the inducting school of social work takes responsibility? As a program of study specifically designed for teachers and prospective teachers in schools of social work as an alternative to doctoral study? Some of the immediately apparent problems of such programs are: Where would they be located? Where would their faculties come from? Would they draw off faculty needed to conduct doctoral programs? Would they attract students who might make a greater contribution to the profession after full doctoral study?

Certainly no plan to develop teachers for schools of social work should result in a one-sided emphasis on the *how* of teaching at the expense of the *what* of teaching and the *who*, in the largest developmental sense, of the teacher.

Whatever the plan, program, method, or process used to develop teaching competence for schools of social work, *commitment* to teaching is a constant requirement. The good teacher likes to see people grow, and to help them grow; he has capacity for relationship with a wide variety of students. The good teacher must combine capacity and motivation for continuing self-development as a scholar and professional person with motivation, knowledge, and skill to put that self at the service of his students toward the end of their learning and becoming.

Some teachers are so great in themselves, so on fire with enthusiasm, that only the greenest timber fails to burn on contact. But certainly, association with genius is not the only way to learn; the student is helped to learn by any teacher who cares about him and his learning, and who has mastered learning and teaching theory and has developed teaching skill.

Capacity for Continuing Self-Development as a Teacher

The good teacher has the interest, motivation, and capacity to experiment

20

with new ways and forms of teaching, as well as to exploit ever more fully the old ways which have historically proved their worth. This implies the continuous acquisition and application of knowledge to improve skill as a teacher, but it does not imply a "flight to the new" just because it is new.

Capacity to Function as a Faculty Member

The good teacher has the capacity to function cooperatively as a member of the faculty "team"; to make his individual contribution as an individual, but in relation to the contributions of his colleagues, as part of a whole, under the discipline of working toward a shared and common purpose. It is an old problem: how to be creative within a pattern; how to be original without being destructive; how to be conscientious, responsible, and related, and still retain a lively spark of individuality and difference.

. . . IN GRADUATE SCHOOLS OF SOCIAL WORK

Identification with the Social Work Profession

Faculty who are professional social workers will have committed themselves to social work, to its values and purposes and their implementation through methods peculiarly appropriate to the profession, before entering teaching. This commitment will have been made as a result of both education and experience. Members of social work faculties who come from other disciplines may never develop an equal depth of identification with the profession. However, the values of faculty from other disciplines—sociology, psychology, psychiatry, or whatever—must not be *incompatible* with the values of social work. Faculty from other disciplines must be convinced of the significance of social work in contemporary life (and hence the significance of education for it) if they are to contribute to it as members of a faculty of a school of social work. The knowledge and perspective they bring to it by being *from*, and to some extent *on*, the "outside," can be enriching if these are used in contributive rather than competitive or insulated ways.

The practice of any profession, but especially social work, requires devotion, discipline, and zest for going beyond the call of duty or the "terms of employment" for what one deeply believes is an important endeavor. The student catches this enthusiasm in the course of being taught. His own zest and devotion to what he is engaged in are quickened and made firm through association with dedicated teachers. Social work faculty commonly and desirably engage in professional as well as scholarly activity, thus reinforcing and giving substance to their teaching and their scholarly work.

Intensive and Extensive Knowledge of a Core Subject Area or Sequence

It has been well said that nothing is more pathetic than a teacher who has nothing to teach. But the knowledge of the social work teacher, while extensive and deep within at least one area or sequence, ideally equips him to teach in more than one, and certainly to be acquainted with and respect the value of, all areas and their place in the total curriculum of preparation for the practice of social work.

Experience in social work practice adds a dimension to social work teaching which only "playing for real" can give. For the teaching of practice it is, of course, a requirement. And that means experience of substance, range, diversity, and considerable duration in some social work process or processes and within several fields of practice.

Use of Generic Principles of Social Work Method in Teaching

This does not mean that the teacher "case works" or "group works" or "community organizes" his students; it means that his understanding or "diagnosis" of his students is related to their promise and problems in using his class toward becoming professional social workers. It means that *as a teacher* he uses what he knows *as a social worker* about engaging in a process of human relationship in such a way that the other is freed and helped to do something constructive within it toward fulfilling his own purpose as it coincides with the purpose of the social institution making a service available. In a school of social work, the service is social work education. The point is that the social work teacher is expected to make *relevant* application of the methods of social work. While any teacher may use identical principles, either intuitively or through the relevant application of methods learned in a different discipline, the social work teacher may rightfully be expected to use and develop as part of his teaching skill what is his through his own social work education. The use of generic principles of social work method does not by any means constitute his *whole* teaching skill. Teaching is a skill in its own right, but the use of generic principles of social work method can contribute appreciably to that skill.

ATTRIBUTES OF FIELD TEACHERS
IN SCHOOLS OF SOCIAL WORK

Field teachers are of two kinds in the present-day practice of social work education: agency supervisors who are serving as field supervisors for a school of social work, and faculty members who are serving as field supervisors of students in an agency or agencies.

Ideally, both groups would share the attributes listed for class faculty, with less scholarship expected or required of them than commitment to, and knowledge and skill in, social work practice and field supervision methods.

22

For both class and field teachers, identification with the functional role of social work teacher is imperative. However, the particular functional role of field teacher involves knowledge and teaching skill, which is in some respects distinctive to field teaching. In addition, a field teacher must have a thorough knowledge of how to make a particular social service available in ways that are of maximum benefit to individual clients and to social welfare in general. His educational responsibility requires that the field teacher be knowledgeable about the school's expectations of all students upon graduation, the pace generally characteristic of students' movement toward the objective of graduation and how that movement is reflected in field learning, and the contribution of the field to the realization of the school's educational objectives. The field supervisor must also develop skill in helping individual students to use their field experience, including the relationship with the field supervisor, to achieve their and the school's objectives (this skill involves a sense of timing).

What is appropriate field learning and teaching at each stage of the two-year program? For each particular student in each particular agency, within the framework of what is possible and required for all students, whatever their placement, field teaching requires a capacity to see the generic in the specific and to abstract the general principle from specific situations and cases. It requires skill in enabling the student to grasp the general principles of helping or functioning in the specific situation, the more readily to use them in succeeding cases, or situations.

The faculty field supervisor may be expected to have an advantage in teaching skill, knowledge of educational objectives, program, and process, and in capacity to see and abstract general principles from specific situations. His particular difficulty will be to represent agency service and to give it in a way that is accountable to agency, community, and clientele while providing the student with the opportunity to be a real social worker in a real situation with real administrative demands and requirements.

The agency field supervisor, on the other hand, has the special advantage of identification with agency service. He represents it as an employee of the agency, responsible for seeing that service is given effectively, helpfully, and with accountability. Such commitment on the part of the supervisor increases the educational value of the agency experience for the student, who feels and responds to the expectation created by the agency's responsibility to give service. The problem for the agency supervisor lies in his relationship to the school's total program and its expectations of its students. He must also learn to see the abstract in the concrete, the general principle in the specific situation, and develop skill in teaching methods appropriate to field work supervision.

So the faculty field teacher must learn to represent a specific agency as one manifestation of social welfare purpose within which the student can

23

learn generic skill and within which he can truly become a social worker in purpose and commitment as well as in skill.

And the agency field supervisor needs to gain perspective on his agency's service as one manifestation of social welfare purpose, to identify its opportunities for student learning as part of a total experience in social work education, and to develop sufficient teaching skill to enable the student to learn, not through apprenticeship, but through a field placement that is consciously, continuously, and knowingly maintained as a vital part of a total program and process of graduate education for social work.

DEVELOPING THE FACULTY:
THE OPPORTUNITIES AND DEMANDS
OF TEACHING*

by Dame Eileen L. Younghusband

(Although addressed to an international audience, Dame Younghusband's perspective may serve for educators in schools in the United States and Canada both as an affirmation of concepts applicable regardless of country, and as a reminder that there may be as much difference between the schools on the North American continent as between schools on other continents; some are stronger, some more sophisticated, and some struggling to get started. In obtaining cues to qualities and preparation needed by all educators, it is important to bear in mind that students after graduation work in different locales and countries. Ed.)

THE NEED FOR GIFTED TEACHERS

The expansion of social work education has led to an almost universal shortage of social workers with the experience, education, and personal qualities needed to become school faculty members or to take responsibility for in-service training. No one is in a more crucial position in relation to the whole development of the social work profession than the teachers of social work. It is primarily they who must transmit to the coming generation of students professional values, clarity about the changing purpose of social work, and much of the knowledge and way of working that underlies professional practice. The faculty of a school of social work is also called upon or expected, in many local or national situations, to give a lead in movements for social reform and social action. And it is they, more than anyone else, who must undertake the research, study, inquiry, and hard thinking needed to extend the range and flexibility of social work method and to bring new knowledge from the behavioral sciences within the ambit of practice. This is all the more necessary at a time when social work is still

---

* Paper presented at the Thirteenth International Congress of Schools of Social Work, September, 1965, in Washington, D. C. as part of the Marie-Louise Ginet and Marjorie Brown Memorial Lecture. (Marie-Louise Ginet of France and Marjorie Brown of Scotland were both directors of schools of social work and leaders in international social work education.) Dame Younghusband was, at that time, president of the International Association of Schools of Social Work. She has also been Advisor on Social Work Training of the National Institute for Social Work Training, London, England.

a fluid and emerging profession, hardly clear about its central purpose and certainly not clear about its boundaries or all its methods.

The social work faculty thus should be a body of gifted teachers, with sure roots in their own profession, a commitment to its aims that encourages an open mind about its practice, together with a zest for their subject and for helping students to learn.

If we think about the great teachers we have known, certain characteristics spring to our minds. All great teachers have in common a charismatic quality of personality which deeply influences students' attitudes. They are always highly individual people; they and their subject have become fused with each other; they are conscious of richness and depth denied to our more limited vision; and they enjoy what A. N. Whitehead called "the habitual vision of greatness." They are great teachers just because they are able to gladden us with their more piercing insight, because inspiration willy-nilly engulfs us as we share vicariously in their ability to win new knowledge with patient integrity of purpose. In short, as we listen to them we realize that we are in the presence of wisdom. There are few such teachers to be met in a lifetime. Let us therefore be grateful for the exceptionally good, even if they fall short of the truly great. With them, too, their most marked characteristic is that their commitment to their subject is not a drudgery but a joy. They are steeped in it and in all that relates to it because it is a central purpose in their lives. And for this same reason they want to communicate it to others. It is this double enthusiasm for knowledge and for its communication through teaching which distinguishes the creative teacher from the pure scholar. The teacher wants students to share his satisfaction in the different dimensions of his subject, wants to see them develop understanding and imagination about it. Thus, he has a strong desire to transmit it to others, to understand how people learn, how to start where they are and thus get across to them so that they in turn may master the subject, make it part of themselves, with the result that it goes on maturing and illuminating their understanding long after they have ceased to be students. Thus, the distinguishing mark of the gifted teacher is this double capacity for absorption in the subject and in the students' development; in short, an ability to create the conditions in which learning takes place. In the last resort it is the personality of the teacher, what he and his subject have become in combination, through which students learn. In addition, any fruitful educational institution is a society in which students and teachers are both learning together.

It is such institutions which make education a continuing process of growth in succeeding years. This level of education in turn produces some people who always want to learn more, to use old knowledge as a springboard for new knowledge, who are eternally curious about the possible relations between A and B, who begin to know what are the right questions

26

to ask and the way to search for answers, who are able to remain flexible, humble, imaginative, and capable of surprise. This is indeed to have the intellectual integrity which in due time may lead to wisdom. Such growth in education also results in greater commitment to certain values fundamental to social work, values related to the importance of ordinary people's well-being, the need not to have any illusions and yet not to become disillusioned. It is indeed the ability to go on liking the human race, even in its least likeable, most damaged, and most sorrowful manifestations, just because it is human.

THE NEED FOR FACULTY DEVELOPMENT

All this sounds very grandiose. It is difficult to talk about great teachers, the purpose of education, or the ideals of social work without seeming to leave the hard realities of everyday life and ordinary people. Yet less than ordinary people, extremely harsh realities, and limited resources are the boundaries within which the primary task of social work must be performed. This task is centered not only in action which arises from people's sheer lack of material resources but also in any circumstances where they suffer from inability to establish satisfying human relationships within the contemporary patterns of society. In pursuance of this task, both social work educators and field instructors must strive to be clear about goals but flexible about methods. It is also a continuing purpose of a school of social work to educate each generation of students better than the one before so that they may see more clearly the changing implications of the social work task and be better prepared to fulfill this task. If these are the aims for a school of social work and the quality of teaching that students should receive, it is possible to argue that such teachers are born not made. But it is equally possible to be astonished that we have only very recently begun to think it necessary to prepare social workers for teaching. The days are past when we thought that someone with rich natural qualities for social work needed no training. This must hold good for teaching too, for no gifted teachers, however great their potentialities, just grew, and less gifted teachers are all the more in need of help if they are to learn to teach students as well as to teach subjects. As Dr. John W. Gardner pungently puts it: "They cannot content themselves with the time-honored process of stuffing students like sausages or even the possibly more acceptable process of training them like seals."[1]

The curriculum studies which have been undertaken by many schools of social work in recent years show the importance of being more alive to edu-

---

[1] John W. Gardner, *Excellence: Can we be Equal and Excellent too?* (New York: Harper and Row, 1961), p. 143.

cational principles. Some make a real contribution to improved social work education, but others tend to move along the single dimension of curriculum content only and to ignore the other dimension of educational principles and methods, the psychology of learning and the philosophy of education. Some curriculum revision has resulted in still further overloading the program because it has not been preceded by a realistic assessment of objectives. It is a time-consuming and difficult task to study the actual demands on social workers in a given country, whether avowed, implicit, or over today's horizon; to relate this to the real needs of the situation, tomorrow as well as today, and to use these findings to determine what should be the objectives of the total educational progam, and thus be used as the guide to curriculum planning. But unless this is done, the school's program will neither be creatively related to the current needs of social agencies nor designed to advance future practice, whether in direct field work or administration and planning. The objectives of the curriculum are also likely to be too diffuse to enable students to absorb and use what they learn.

The case for planned faculty development, teaching the teacher how to teach, thus rests upon the assumption that both teaching and curriculum planning are complex activities for which systematic learning and practice are needed. Unfortunately, at present, the newly appointed teacher is usually left to learn by trial and error at the expense of the students. It is indeed true that the teacher can only ultimately learn from the students, that teaching is a relationship in which sensitivity to the impact on the learner is essential for success as a teacher. But to rely on this without the guidance which knowledge can give is an unnecessarily slow process, full of errors for the teacher and trials for the students, and moreover with an uncertain outcome because bad teaching methods, irrelevant or inappropriate content, mistakes in presentation, and failures in response to group feeling may become ingrained.

We are indignant when it is suggested that members of some other profession would be equally competent to carry out a social work function. But why do we think that a social worker should be competent to teach students, often with a minimum of time for preparation of the course content or for study, and with no training in educational principles and methods?

THE INTERNATIONAL PERSPECTIVE

Since we are an international gathering, it is also necessary to think about the varied tasks which face social work educators in different parts of the world because of differences in the level of social development and the cultural values of their countries, together with the differing educational backgrounds and degree of maturity of the students. For example, a school of social work may face its students with acute conflict if it successfully pre-

28

pares them for a level of practice and degree of insight far removed from that of existing social agencies and the values of their particular culture. A group of professionally conscious and intelligent social work educators said recently: "In our culture it is we who are the maladjusted." They recognized with painful frustration that their educational aims, which are based upon freedom of thought and discussion, critical analysis, capacity for problem-solving, and respect for the individual's essential right to make decisions about his own life, were deeply at variance with attitudes in their society as expressed in the educational system and public social agencies. But if social work students are simply taught to become faithful retriever dogs for administrators, they will hardly fulfill social work's role as a precipitator and shock absorber of social change and its more fundamental role in humanizing social relationships.

The art of social work education may be all the more difficult to practice in those parts of the world where students, who are often inexperienced young women, may come from small town backgrounds in which it is customary to accept rigid codes of behavior and to mistake prejudice for universally binding morality. Such students may also have had a school experience based upon rote learning and unquestioning acceptance of what the teacher told them. In many of the world's schools the old static concept continues that education consists of facts to be learned by heart. This is a poor preparation for scientific study and personal responsibility in a world of flux and change. A class of adolescent girls straight from an authoritarian school system with a tradition-oriented cultural background, perhaps centered in a pre-scientific world outlook, poses acute problems for the social work teacher. These problems are different from those which face his colleague in another part of the world responsible for a class of older postgraduate students with a future-oriented outlook who have been educated in the atmosphere of critical analysis and scientific inquiry characteristic of a modern university. This latter teacher may not face an easy task in educating the heart as well as the head or in keeping the balance true between academic and professional learning. But here the starting point, the educational methods, and goal will be very different from those of the other social work educator who must make up deficiencies in basic education, help students to master the elements of learning, including the ability for independent study and to be able to discuss and think for themselves, even to become conscious that the moral code in which they have been brought up may be too rigid to meet the diversities of human need and human values in a changing world. Such students also face a hard task in accepting the variety of human behavior with a view to trying to understand contributory causation and motivation rather than in terms of moral stereotypes of good or bad behavior. For them the cultural shock of self-awareness may equal the personal emotional turmoil. They will go through more stress too than

29

university graduates in learning to live with the uncertainty induced by discovering that there are no neat answers in the behavioral sciences.

Social work teachers, indeed, face a difficult task in helping students from such backgrounds to achieve, without too great personal damage, a compassionate awareness of themselves and others and ability for dispassionate thought. This task is far more difficult than in those societies where the ancient Greeks, Dr. Freud, and social mobility have had a more pervasive influence. In short, what the social work educator can hope to achieve over a given period of time is largely affected by the age, type of educational experience, and family and cultural background from which the students come. Nonetheless, the cultivation of social sensitivity combined with professional self-discipline is no easy endeavor with any group of students.

All this may seem far removed from the subject of faculty development. But we cannot think profitably about the preparation of social work educators without taking account of the nature of the task, who are the students, what is the role and function for which they are being prepared in the given circumstances of a particular society, and what professional values and objectives should be. This means accepting that students must be able to practice usefully in given situations immediately after graduation but must also be agents of change, not only amongst their clients but in the social agencies which employ them. Furthermore, there are some situations in which the need for well-educated and appropriately trained social administrators, policy makers, and planners is greater than that for qualified field practitioners working directly with clients.

ESSENTIAL STEPS IN THE PREPARATION OF FACULTY

No matter what the circumstances, the students' background, and the nature of the curriculum, there are several essential requirements which should be observed in appointing faculty members of schools of social work. The first is that they should have a real desire to teach and to be responsible for students' development, with the accompanying solid grounding in their subject and the intellectual integrity which teaching demands. They themselves should be well-educated social workers who have put what they have learned to the test of practice in their own country. In some situations those who have qualified in another part of the world return immediately to teach. This is only tolerable for a short period at a pioneer stage in the country's development when no other alternative is possible. In any event, no one without a satisfactory professional qualification as a social worker should teach social work practice. Moreover, it is essential that all social work teachers should be able to read fluently one of the languages in which current social work and related literature is available. These are sometimes tough but always necessary minimum requirements.

The next step is to think out what new teachers need by way of systematic preparation for the change from social work practice to social work teaching. There are various ways of providing this preparation. One possibility is to attach the newly appointed teacher to an experienced faculty member for regular discussion about the planning of the particular course, its objectives, its content, and the most effective educational methods to use; as well as for systematic thought about the students' responses and learning as the course proceeds. A better alternative is to appoint a consultant in faculty development who will work with several schools and hold seminars in relevant subjects. Another alternative is the provision of national or regional seminars from time to time. This possibility will be discussed later. Perhaps the most satisfactory of all is to initiate substantial full- or part-time courses of related theory and practice for former social work practitioners who are changing to or already engaged in social work teaching.

Experience indicates that there is a certain common content needed by all new social work teachers, and that the program should consist of related theory and practice. An important initial step is to help the former social worker begin to think in educational terms rather than social work terms but to do this by changing the focus from the one to the other. Much social work knowledge and some of its competence are relevant to the educational situation but they must be shifted into an educational frame of reference with educational assessment, diagnosis, and problem-solving as the guide and educational achievement as the goal. It is sometimes not easy for social workers to make this shift, to become clear that their primary objective is the education of the students rather than therapy.

Another essential step is to stretch the new social work teacher's imagination and understanding about the social work function and its actual or potential contribution to current social welfare policies, which are themselves changing in the broader context of social development. This will inevitably include trying to think out what newly qualified students from a school of social work should know and be able to do, what values and ability to practice they must have as a basis for beginning as social workers in the particular circumstances of their country. These objectives cast light on the desirable nature and content of the curriculum and the particular educational goals of the new teacher in relation to the total learning process. He must be stimulated to do some hard thinking about the evolving nature of social work, its contribution to social development, the equipment of the newly qualified social worker, and the touchstone which this provides for deciding the objectives of social work education. This is the right order of priorities rather than planning the content of a course of study without reference to its objectives and their relation to the students' learning capacity. This ability to learn is not only connected with their educational

31

and cultural background but also with the astonishing differences, variations, and fluctuations in individual motivation, about which we know comparatively little.

It is essential that social work teachers should struggle to come to grips with these different issues, bringing to bear upon them knowledge, imagination, and a sense of the possible. In doing this they will naturally use existing studies of social work practice, of curriculum planning and educational method. Most systematic studies have been done in the United States, which means that they do not necessarily apply in their totality elsewhere, and they are certainly not to be studied for passive acceptance. Their value lies in clarifying some principles of action, but hard work is needed to understand these principles and to translate them into relevant learning experiences elsewhere.

Attempts to plan the social work curriculum, and the place of any given course in it, in the light of objectives for beginning social work performance, should result in some drastic pruning in order to arrive at manageable objectives, considered from the point of view of time, resources, and the students' abilities. This is also a salutory exercise in deciding learning priorities, in thinking about educational processes and student motivation, about organizing principles or core concepts, and how to sustain disciplined curiosity rather than swamping students with what A. N. Whitehead calls "inert knowledge," that is to say, knowledge which they cannot quickly put to use and which therefore evaporates.

As part of the means to these ends a social work educator must learn to ask some of the following questions about his teaching: "Will this particular knowledge be used in social work practice? If so, how?" "What do I expect the students to be able to do with this material or experience? And are sufficient opportunities provided for learning to use it, whether for understanding or practice?" "How much is enough, or too little or too much?" "What are the connecting threads or guiding principles that must run all through the curriculum so that the diversity and amount of knowledge becomes coherent and usable?" "What understanding is available about the psychology of learning, about educational method, communication, group relations, and student motivation which would speed up and intensify the whole process of learning and of growth to greater professional maturity?" "And how can this be done without causing the students mental indigestion or malnutrition?" In short: "How can they be actively engaged in the learning process?"

Obviously these are the kind of questions which do not have neat answers. They are questions which suggest that some lines of action are more fruitful than others. They also imply that any attempt to prepare would-be social work teachers must move all the time along the two dimensions of content and method. A little has been said already about the content. An additional value of a substantial course of study for social work teachers is to give them time and opportunity for reading, time to become immersed in the best current writing and thought in the social and behavioral sciences, social welfare, and social work. This study has the double aim of increasing the social work teacher's own knowledge and understanding in relation to how, when, and for what purpose particular content should be used in teaching; and also to enable him to think out appropriate guidance for students' independent study.

Every social work educator needs to be intelligently knowledgeable about the subjects taught by social scientists and other specialists in a school of social work. This is necessary for discussion with them about those aspects of their subjects which are relevant or not relevant for social work students. It is also essential for teachers of social work practice to use social science and other knowledge in their own teaching. Thus, a major purpose of a period of systematic study is to give them opportunity and guidance in preparing the courses which they themselves will teach, as well as to study other related subjects.

Opportunities for practice are as necessary in this type of program as in social work education itself. Social work teachers not only need a seminar on the content, methods of presentation, organizing principles, and objectives of social work and other courses which they may teach, but also actual teaching practice with a group of students for whom they have full responsibility. Ideally they should record in process some class sessions and subsequently discuss them with an experienced faculty member, bringing out what they taught and why, how the class reacted, how they dealt with difficult situations, and what the members seemed to need and to learn.

One of the most important tasks of a school of social work is to help its students to relate theory to practice. This means teaching those aspects of theory most relevant to practice in its broadest sense and also providing opportunities for practice which make it possible to relate them to each other in a systematic way. A course for social work teachers must therefore provide opportunities for studying key aspects of field teaching in social work education, its importance for professional practice, its relation to classroom teaching, and what this means for the faculty member who has an educational responsibility for supervisors, some of whom may not even be qualified social workers, and in any event frequently do not have sufficient time to give to students. This study of field teaching and learning is equally necessary when the school faculty undertakes student supervision.

TEACHING THE TEACHERS

In planning a course for social work teachers, one is struck by the dearth of good studies on how adults learn, the kind of study which would give guidance on the most effective curriculum planning, educational methods, and learning experiences to use in social work education. Of course there is much generally accepted knowledge about the psychology of learning which applies equally to children and adults. Nonetheless the teaching of adults differs in obvious ways from the teaching of children.

It is vital to keep constantly in mind that imaginative consideration lies at the heart of education. We must always be conscious that our aim is not to impart a series of techniques to be applied mechanically but to enable would-be teachers to think more profoundly and to better purpose, to stretch their imagination, with the aid of knowledge, and to help each one to discover his own best way of communicating his understanding of social work to students.

If social work faculty members ought to have some or all of the learning experiences discussed earlier, the next question is how to provide this for them. . . . It has been suggested that the most satisfactory solution would be long-term courses consisting of class discussion, individual tutorial help, opportunities for study and observation and with related teaching practice. Another possibility is to hold periodic seminars for faculty members who are already teaching in a group of schools. Where neither this nor the appointment of a faculty development consultant is possible, another solution would be a planned teaching/learning attachment to a faculty member in a good school of social work at home or abroad. Another possibility is to run regional seminars for social work faculty members.

Undoubtedly the ideal would be to combine a variety of different methods for faculty development. In addition to those already discussed, more help might be given by means of written materials for those who are already teaching, though there is the risk that these would only speak to those who have the experience to hear what they say. It is also possible that tape recordings of various elements in faculty development would be useful, for example, recordings of class sessions, with teaching notes on the content and method of presentation.

Various means of teaching the teachers must be pioneered, whether in isolation or combination. The first step is to reach agreement on the need for faculty development. Indeed we must recognize that the proper preparation of social work teachers is a vital element in solving the problem of how to expand the number of qualified social workers to meet manpower shortages without at the same time sacrificing quality. Quantity is a crucial issue at the present time but quality is, if anything, still more crucial.

The ranks of social work educators are continually replenished and expanded by new members who were themselves the students of a previous generation. Yet in a profession as fluid as social work, what these new teachers need is not static knowledge from the past but pioneering attitudes and a zest for knowledge and its application that will match the tasks of the future. Beyond all this, they need to be people who can inspire students to see today the challenge of tomorrow, and who are able to say with the unknown writer: "I cannot teach people to be helping people; I can only help loving persons to express their love more constructively." Without love, in its widest meaning, neither good social work nor good teaching is possible; for without love the fires of creativity burn low.

Yet for all that, love is not enough. We need far more knowledge too, knowledge based upon the social research which is crying out to be done in many different directions. We need, too, ability to turn more scientific knowledge into professional practice, into a wider range of practice than we have encompassed so far.

We who are social work educators from all over the world must realize that unless social work can expand the effective range of its methods so that it can occupy a central place in major endeavors to enrich the quality of social living for normal people, then it will remain a peripheral, if valuable, profession, concentrating its energies on personal help to the deviant and the deprived. At the present time, the outcome hangs in the balance as to whether or not social work will advance, like other professions in their various spheres, to the point where it can make a significant central contribution to improving social relationships for the mass of people, as medicine can improve their health through large-scale public health measures. If we are not able to rise to this challenge, then we shall be left behind by new professions emerging to occupy the place where we could have been.

Social work educators of this generation and that which will succeed us face what will be either a broader road ahead or the parting of the ways. The outcome will depend on the answer we give or fail to give to this challenge. The demands we have to meet are indeed greater than they have ever been before not because we shall fail, but because, given wisdom, we, or our successors, might prove equal to the task.

FOUR COMPONENTS OF PREPARATION FOR THE SOCIAL WORK EDUCATOR

by Joseph Soffen*

(*The following selection identifies four components which social work educators should have to meet the demands of their calling. Although all four are essential, it is proposed that they are needed in varying degrees, depending upon the special interest, aptitude, and career aspiration of each individual. Ed.*)

What is a good teacher? Each level within the educational hierarchy—the administrator, the teacher, and the student—has an idealized model: one who is creative, contributing, inspiring. But these are global qualities and offer no clue to how they can be achieved. It would appear, therefore, that to give direction to what a prospective teacher can do to prepare for a teaching career, some answers are needed to the questions: What are demands of his total range of responsibilities? What should he know and what should he be able to do? Before answering these questions, however, it may be appropriate to review several extant models for the teacher.

THE SCHOLAR AND THE SCHOLARLY PROFESSIONAL

There is no dearth of truly inspiring descriptions of good teaching. Each generation in the history of man has known good teachers and described their qualities. Definitions of a good teacher are often lofty descriptions of an ideal, but an operational definition has continued to be elusive. Some have approached the question by describing *attributes* of a good *teacher*, others the *qualities* of good *teaching*; some probe for the essence of creativity. Some are confident that the definition of good teaching will emerge as we gain greater understanding of good learning. Gardner is reassuring when he observes that "the mercurial spirit of great teaching and great scholarship cannot be organized, rationalized, delegated, or processed."[1] Without presuming to review all that has been said about good teachers and good teaching, we

---

[1] John Gardner, *Self-Renewal: The Individual and the Innovative Society* (New York: Harper and Row, 1963), p. 82.

---

* A shortened version of Chapter 4 of *Faculty Development in Professional Education* (New York: Council on Social Work Education, 1967). Dr. Soffen is on the faculty of the School of Social Work, University of Pennsylvania.

should note briefly a few sources which may be representative of the current state of the question before adjusting the focus on the social work teacher.

Diekhoff conceives of "scholar teachers" who may be "productive scholars" and others who may be "productive teachers":

> If his love of learning results in the continuing increase of [his own] knowledge, that is as it should be. If it leads him to increase not only his own but also the world's knowledge, he is what we call a "productive scholar." If his love of learning leads him to share his knowledge and his love of it with others, we may call him a "productive teacher."

> It is commonplace to regard productive scholarship and productive teaching as mutually exclusive accomplishments, perhaps no product of the graduate school is more likely to be an effective college teacher than the productive scholar, not because "productive scholarship" is a condition of good teaching but because love of learning is a condition of both scholarship and teaching. The real enthusiast for knowledge will pursue it and will communicate it, in books and articles or in the classroom, or by both means.

> Of course there are scholars who do not publish. We have called them "productive teachers." They may be the best teachers we have. But failure to publish is not what makes them good teachers, and it does not follow that a faculty member is a good teacher because he does not publish. He is not likely to be a good teacher unless he shares the enthusiasm for knowledge of the productive scholar.[2]

Lamenting what he observes to be a decline in the role of the teacher-scholar for whom there is "less and less prestige," Riesman describes him as:

> ... a person who regards himself as a reflective and civilized student of his subject without feeling he must do extensive research in it. There never were many such people on the American academic scene, and the majority of professors . . . who claimed to be scholars were either ham actors, or pedants, or both. But the scholar is not . . . part of an academic production line so much as the man who reads and reflects and enjoys learning and in the continuing debate on research versus teaching, this particular species tends to drop from view.[3]

Apparently, with the same model in mind, Brown lists as the attributes of the creative teacher-scholar: an inquiring mind, the powers of analysis and accumulation, intuition, self-discipline, and a tendency toward perfectionism. The last attribute may be expected to be associated with tendencies to introspection and to resistance to external authority.[4]

---

[2] John S. Diekhoff, The Domain of the Faculty (New York: Harper and Brothers), pp. 52-53.

[3] David Riesman, "Alterations in Institutional Attitudes and Behavior," in Logan Wilson, ed., Emerging Patterns in American Higher Education (Washington, D. C.: American Council on Education, 1965), p. 68.

[4] J. Douglas Brown, "The Development of Creative Teacher-Scholars," Daedalus (Summer, 1965), pp. 615-631.

In an incisive critique of American higher education, Sanford uses an anthropological frame of reference to classify teachers. For example, the teacher as "shaman" may be "vain or exhibitionistic . . . [or] withdrawn, diffident, even humble. Essentially, however, he keeps the audience's attention focused on himself. He invites us to observe the personality in its encounter with the subject matter. . . . When this orientation is combined with unusual gifts, we have a charismatic teacher . . . marked by power, energy, and commitment." The teacher as priest "stresses not his personal virtues, but his membership in a powerful or admirable collectivity, e.g., physics, psychoanalysis, classical scholarship. . . . [He] says: 'I am valuable for what I belong to. I represent and personify a collective identity.' " A third type is classified as "mystic healer" who is "altruistic," who "concentrates neither on himself, nor on the subject matter, nor the discipline, but on the student saying 'I will help you become what you are.' . . . [He] keeps his own achievement and personality secondary; he works to help the student find what is best and most essential within himself."[5]

Goheen sharpens the concept that is an attribute of the good teacher to focus upon the learner and to interact with him:

> Each great teacher has his own unique way. Yet, more often than not, two particular attributes will be found in the successful teacher. One is an ability to awaken and stimulate delight in the use of the mind. The second is attention to the effort to do so, together with a belief in its value to the student in his own right. . . .
>
> There is another role that the good teacher plays. He is interpreter in the house of learning. Now, the word interpret has several connotations: to explain—to construe. All involve the making of a connection. This is what the teacher does. He puts the student in connection with the problem at hand and leads him to seek and press an engagement with it.[6]

As we turn to the teacher in professional education, we will see some of the qualities of the model of the academic scholar, sometimes in the same terms, sometimes recast.

The Scholarly Professional. These attributes are sharpened, and additional ones are introduced by the unique character of professional education. Thus, the teaching function in legal education according to Freund must be reflective of the following formulation of objectives:

> . . . the transitoriness of a large part of the informational content has forced the schools to a sharper appreciation of what they have always professed, that their mission is not to produce lawyers, but minds trained for law. More specifically, there is an intensified effort to explore fields of law by

---

[5] Nevitt Sanford, The American College (New York: John Wiley and Sons, 1962), pp. 407-412.

[6] Robert F. Goheen, "The Teacher in the University," School and Society, Vol. 94, No. 2276 (April 2, 1966), p. 177.

sinking shafts rather than covering the ground. More basically there is encouragement to seek for common or unifying principles that will help consolidate and simplify. . . .[7]

Or, in nursing education, "the single purpose . . . is to prepare professional nurse practitioners who can command a growing body of knowledge in their nursing practice, clinical care, and services and are able to share, with the physicians and members of the allied professions, a greater responsibility for the welfare of patients and the health of families."[8]

To provide a "perspective on teaching-scholarship" in *teacher education*, Stratemeyer outlines the following dimensions: understanding the power of knowledge to open doors; having insight into significant relationships among ideas, phenomena, and events; differentiating between intensive and extensive study, between awareness as contrasted with understanding-in-depth of situations of human importance. But "to use knowledge intelligently requires more knowing. . . . [It] means zeal for constructive action based on meaningful *inter-relating of thinking, feeling, and behaving.* The relationship between intention and action, insight and courage, vision and drive are factors vital to scholarship today, and mandatory in teaching-scholarship." She adds as a "unique professional dimension" scholarship that includes "having insight into helping others—individuals and groups—develop competence and genuine interest in learning. This characteristic distinguishes teaching-scholarship from that of other professionals."[9]

The teacher-scholar "has the ability to bring personal meaning to the world of ideas. He possesses his own unique framework, he has his own good reasons for learning what he decides to learn. . . . He is able to select and build upon significant ideas, observe relationships and distinguish essential matters from irrelevant and incidental ones."[10]

THE SOCIAL WORK TEACHER

Although the social work curriculum aims at integration of its subject areas, each area has its own characteristics. In turn, faculty members may

---

[7] Paul A. Freund, "The Legal Profession," *Daedalus* (Fall, 1963), p. 698.

[8] Frances Reiter, "The Generic Program of the Graduate School of Nursing of the New York Medical College," in *Nursing Education—Creative, Continuing, Experimental,* papers presented at the Twentieth Conference of the Council of Member Agencies of the Department of Baccalaureate and Higher Degree Programs (New York: National League for Nursing, 1966), p. 11.

[9] Florence B. Stratemeyer, "Perspective on Action in Teacher Education," in *Action for Improvement of Teacher Education,* Eighteenth Yearbook (Washington: American Association of Colleges for Teacher Education, 1965), pp. 23-41.

[10] Dean Corrigan, "The Personal Dimension in the Education of American Teachers," paper prepared for the conference honoring Florence B. Stratemeyer, French Lick, Indiana, June 10-12, 1965.

become identified with one or another of the curricular areas. Ideally each will not only see the relationship of his area to the whole but help the student see the mutual interrelationships of the social work methods, social-psychological, social welfare policy, and research sequences. The question remains, however, whether differential preparation and experience is appropriate or whether there should be one typology.

Boehm conjectures about alternative patterns, patterns analogous to those developing in other professional schools.

> Should social work faculty members be engaged in teaching what may in time become the basic social work sciences, as well as social work values and the social work methods, or should different faculty personnel be employed for these two components of the curriculum? Certainly a case could be made for either pattern.
>
> . . . Conceivably two sets of social work faculty might be developed, both recruited from social work, with one group teaching in the foundation component, and the other group in the methods components of the curriculum.[11]

He suggests two additional possible patterns: "that social worker personnel teach the methods courses, and that the basic social science areas be taught by faculty recruited from those fields . . ."; or, that "there be clinical teachers who would collaborate in their clinical teaching with scientific personnel drawn partly from social work and partly from the underlying social and biological sciences."

Jennings found four current types of social work faculty, models partly synthesized from the ideal types described in the general literature of higher education. The four types are: the teacher-social worker; the academic scholar; the research-consultant; and the professor-administrant.[12]

The goals of the social work curriculum place a high level of expectation on the educator.

> Educators [for the profession] endeavor to develop a high level of competence for immediate use. . . . It is a characteristic of professional education that it teaches a body of principles and concepts for differential use. It should foster . . . the inclination to understand these principles beyond the confines of the profession. In short, it endeavors to set in operation a learning process that will endure and wax strong throughout the years of professional activity.

---

[11] Werner W. Boehm, ed., *Objectives of the Social Work Curriculum*, Vol. 1, *Social Work Curriculum Study* (New York: Council on Social Work Education, 1959), pp. 214-215.

[12] Daniel Jennings, "Characteristics of Faculty Members at Graduate Professional Schools of Social Work in the United States and Canada" (Unpublished doctoral dissertation, Catholic University, 1965), pp. 52-53. See also, "Characteristics of Social Work Faculty Members," *Social Work Education Reporter*, Vol. 14, No. 3 (September, 1966), pp. 23 ff.

Thus professional education trains for professional self-dependence. There cannot be an admixture of limited goals and high goals. . . .[13]

Towle partializes these high goals into five categories of aims:

To develop in students the capacity to think critically and analytically and to synthesize and to generalize. . . .

To develop feelings and attitudes that will make it possible for the student to think and act appropriately. . . .

To develop a capacity for establishing and sustaining purposeful working relationships. . . .

To develop social consciousness and social conscience . . . to which are subsidiary a critical, rather than worshipful, attitude toward the profession's rationale and instruments . . . a constructively critical attitude both toward society's response to the profession and toward the profession's principles and instruments. . . .

To develop an orientation to the place of the profession in the society in which it operates. . . .[14]

Smalley first lists five desirable attributes for *all teachers in graduate schools*: an "interesting" self in lively possession of its own uniqueness as an individual; scholarly qualities; skill in teaching and commitment to teaching; interest, motivation, and capacity for continuing the development of himself as a teacher; and capacity to function as a member of a faculty—to develop his own knowledge and his own teaching skill, to make his own contribution as an individual but as part of a whole working toward a shared and common purpose.

For *social work* faculty, she adds: identification with the profession for which the school is preparing; knowledge of range and depth within a particular core subject area or sequence; commitment to the use and continuing development of skill in the generic principles of social work method. . . .[15]

Identifying "an ability to create the conditions in which learning takes place" as an essential quality of skill in teaching for social work, Younghusband asserts:

Any fruitful educational institution is a society in which students and teachers are both learning together.

It is such institutions which make education a continuing process of growth in succeeding years. This level of education in turn produces some

---

[13] Charlotte Towle, *The Learner in Education for the Professions* (Chicago: University of Chicago Press, 1954), pp. 5-6.

[14] *Ibid.*, pp. 6-17.

[15] Ruth E. Smalley, "The Attributes of a Social Work Educator." Reprinted in this volume, pp. 18-24.

people who always want to learn more, to use old knowledge as a springboard for new knowledge, who are eternally curious . . . who begin to know what are the right questions to ask and the way to search for answers, who are able to remain flexible, humble, imaginative, and capable of surprise. This is indeed to have the intellectual integrity which in due time may lead to wisdom.[16]

Finally, since "the process of discovering knowledge, not the acquiring of authorized information" must be one of the outcomes of social work education, "we must enable our students to learn the process of learning in order to contribute effectively, not merely to survive. . . ."[17]

The listing of aims and the formulation of categories of attributes are a useful beginning. But it is essential to take the next, more difficult step before proposing how these attributes are to be achieved. It is necessary to be precise about *what the social work educator must know* and *how much*, and *what he must be able to do* and *how well*. (The reader may agree with our conclusion that the continuing debates about preparation for teaching in higher education, to which we have referred, have been unresolved precisely because of the surprising lack of attention given to this essential intermediate step.)

Two sets of attributes are noted but need no further discussion here. The first set deals with the personal, charismatic qualities, e.g., enthusiasm, individuality, "personality," magnetism. They may be considerations in choosing a faculty career or in being selected for one, but they are possibly end products of a depth of knowing and wisdom about which we are not sufficiently knowledgeable,[18] and therefore are not included as a component of preparation. Similarly, the value system that a social work educator brings to his university calling must be appropriate and beyond question. When more is known about how professional values are acquired and strengthened, these may well be included as a component of preparation. For the time being, a high degree of assurance is to be found in the fact that the social worker brings with him a system of professional values congruent with those of the professional educator. At any rate, the questions of "how much" of professional values and "for whom" do not require discussions; the answers are obvious.

There are four components other than the charismatic and values compo-

[16] Dame Eileen L. Younghusband, "Developing the Faculty: The Opportunities and Demands of Teaching." Reprinted in this volume, pp. 25-35.

[17] William H. Barber, "Keynote Address," in *Remaking the World of the Career Teacher* (Washington, D. C.: National Education Association of the United States, 1966), pp. 35-36.

[18] See, for example, *Daedalus* (Summer, 1965), especially articles by David Hawkins, "The Informed Vision," pp. 538-552, and Jerome Kagan, "Personality and the Learning Process," pp. 553-563.

nents which constitute the preparatory equipment of the social work teacher. The four components are: (1) the subject matter areas of social work and social welfare, (2) the practice of social work, (3) research in social work and social work education, and (4) teaching. These categories have been somewhat arbitrarily formulated for convenience of exposition.

Each of the component areas must further be partialized. There are degrees of knowledge—knowledge about an area of subject matter, knowledge in depth, and knowledge for use. Upon the latter, choices based on values are made, and priorities are set. There is wisdom, which is knowledge tested in the crucible of experience. Each component has analogous levels. There is knowledge about practice, skill in practice (with its own several levels), and practice wisdom. One can be a sophisticated consumer of research, he can understand research methodology, or he may have research skill. The teaching component, similarly, has knowledge and attitudinal ingredients as well as skill. Professional wisdom is therefore a blending of knowledge, values, and skills not confined to one area of subject matter. The partialization which follows, as an intermediate step for purpose of description, admittedly does violence to the organic quality of the living essence of the great teacher.

The Subject Matter Component

The teaching-learning transaction cannot be conceived of as taking place with inadequate currency in subject matter. The objectives of professional education deal with intellectual as well as attitudinal and skill outcomes. There can be no debate about the place of knowledge in the equipment of the educator. No one responsibly fails to value the subject matter component.

Whether the new faculty member is to meet classroom or field responsibilities, or whether he comes with little or a great deal of experience in practice, he will be handicapped in measuring up to expectations without additional formal substantive education. He will need it to find an effective, creative, and satisfying role for himself on a social work faculty, either for the present or the future. The depth of content will depend upon the area of specialization.

This conclusion does not to any degree imply disrespect for current senior faculty who may not have had formal advanced education. They have, in fact, been among the pioneers and the creators of the new knowledge which now requires additional study by the younger generations.

How much and for whom are questions that are best answered by recognizing that all faculty cannot be expected to be equally prepared in all areas of content. Depth or specialization is inevitable and desirable. Two points are being postulated here: field instructors and teachers of practice need advanced substantive content as well as do teachers in other subject areas. This content cannot currently be acquired either at the master's level or as practice wisdom alone.

The Practice Component

Historically, most social work educators came directly from many years of practice, and the practice component has been taken for granted as basic to the preparation of social work educators. (The conviction in social work education about the importance of this component may, in fact, be one of its contributions to the design for education in other professions.) Despite the accomplishments within social work education, the practice-before-teaching dictum has been re-opened for questioning on the current scene. Some of the questioning may be the result of the pressure for more teachers, and schools have been forced to recruit individuals with very few years of practice experience. The economic consideration should not be discounted; after a few years of experience, the type of social worker who attracts the attention of a school as a potential recruit will have advanced in salary to a point which cannot readily be matched by university salaries for the lower ranks.

The critical question remains how much of the practice component in the preparation for which faculty? Here we find a myriad of positions. One position holds strongly that most, if not all, faculty in education for social work must have a clinical qualification, i.e., an MSW degree and experience in practice. Erudite and otherwise qualified academicians may be able to absorb an approximation of practice sophistication, but it is at best a compromise. Another position partializes, and, while it values the practice-oriented professor, agrees that he is not essential in some areas of curriculum. Surely the teachers in the "Social Work Methods" sequences must have had practice experience, but the scientist, from the academic disciplines which now comprise social work knowledge, has major contributions to make, even without a clinical identification.

One prediction is that the inevitable curriculum of the future will deemphasize clinical experience, at the same time as another sees the emergence of the clinical professor who does his clinical teaching in educational centers, similar to the teaching hospital in medical and nursing education. On the current scene we are witnessing *de facto* applications of each of these positions. Surely it is not our prerogative to foreclose on these developments; none of these positions will (or should) be written off for the foreseeable future. The essential conclusion is that the practice component must be included in planning for the preparation of a not inconsiderable number of the social work educators who will be needed in the future as in the present.

There is currently no evidence about the optimum amount of practice experience as a pre-service requirement before beginning teaching. Most of the schools currently induct new faculty with a range of practice experience. They use different rationales. One point of view notes that the two years of experience in field work which is accounted for at the master's level of professional education should not be discounted. Another point of view is based

44

on the belief that clinical experience can appropriately be obtained in the in-service period.

The Research Component

There is a desperate need for research skill and significant research activity if social work schools are to fulfill their mission for the field and take their appropriate place in the university community. Unfortunately, this postulate is too often presented in a manner which appears either to deny the importance of other educational functions, or to claim that research skill is inclusive of any of the other skills. Again, we must ask: how much research and for whom?

We do not know whether good practitioners can be good researchers or whether good researchers can be good practitioners; whether the skills are independent, whether they complement or crowd each other. The answer may depend on the kind of research one has in mind.

Schools of social work will continue to need both gifted practitioner-teachers and also faculty who are imaginative and skilled researchers. In other words, there is a need for a range of research skills within a faculty; research skill is no more an absolute quality than are any of the other components. Some members of a faculty are expected to be able to initiate major research projects of their own, others to teach research to their students. However, even those who teach in curricular areas other than research, will need basic research sophistication if they are to fulfill the expectations set for them by the social work curriculum for educating practitioners:

> The advancement of learning demands research, ingrained as an attitude of mind in all members and developed as a special skill in some. A research approach to the solution of a problem enables the practitioner to learn through experience and to convey what he learns. Certain knowledge of research and disciplined thinking will make for intelligent interpretation and use of the work of those who are specifically engaged in it. The development within a profession of its own research both improves its service and bespeaks the maturation of the field of endeavor. Sound research proceeds from and contributes to sound practice.[19]

Following through on this line of reasoning, all faculty will in the future need basic research skill and sophistication beyond that attained at the master's level. All will be consumers of research. All will participate in research as teachers, in action-research. The research specialists, the initiators and the independent researchers, will obviously need skill of a much different order.

Neither the basic nor the more advanced levels of knowledge and skill in research, of the quality needed for productive performance by a faculty member, has been assured at the master's level in the past, nor have "third-year"

---

[19] Towle, *op. cit.*, p. 6.

programs stressed this objective. Very few individuals acquire research skill exclusively in agency work. A few schools are currently introducing a research specialization at the master's level (innovations approved by CSWE through its accrediting process) for a small number of students who come with social agency experience, with social work practice skill, a beginning knowledge of research methodology, and with a manifest interest in social work research as a career objective. It is too early to know what the level of research attainment will be. At any rate, the number of future teachers coming through this route is not likely to be large. The argument clearly leads to the conclusion that the several levels of research skill will need to be acquired through educational programs beyond the master's.

In addition to the research courses in advanced and doctoral programs, the dissertation is the traditional means by which research skill is acquired and demonstrated. If it is under attack in certain quarters, it is either because it sometimes does not achieve functionally the research objective, or more frequently because objectives are claimed for the dissertation with which it should not be burdened. It is, probably, an effective means for achieving some research objectives, but *it does not differentiate between objectives for the several levels of research skill needed by the schools.* We take no position about whether it is the only means, or the best means. More important is the fact that it does not deal with the other component objectives of advanced education.

The Teaching Component

The new teacher, eager to fulfill his calling, may know about the attributes, he may be inspired by the exhortations to want to be a good teacher, but they cannot in themselves make him one. They do not tell him what to do so that these can also be *his* attributes.

Granted that the faculty member is adequately prepared with respect to the amount and depth of knowledge which he has made his own, with practice wisdom for making vital that knowledge, and with research sophistication which makes knowledge and wisdom progressive, explorative, and expanding. He must also have the ability to make these resources— which *he* possesses available for use by his students. It is difficult to find a term to delineate this ability. As has been noted, some see teaching as essentially an art, and deny that it can be learned. Others are confident that it can, that the ability to teach is both teachable and learnable. They point to the tremendous accretion of understanding about the teacher-learner transaction, an understanding whose frontier is constantly being expanded. Some of this group therefore call it a science, while others, who also see teaching ability based on a growing body of knowledge, are reluctant to attach the scientific label to it. Still others hyphenate both art *and* science. For our purposes, however, the concept encompasses much more than mechanics or tech-

46

nical skills. It refers to an ability built upon: (1) philosophical foundations, i.e., the purposes and issues of educational thought; (2) psychological foundations, i.e., how the learner learns;[20] and (3) knowledge and skill in communication, in the organization of curriculum, and in the appropriate use of a range of teaching-learning methodologies. Too often taken for granted, but explicitly to be subsumed under these broad formulations of foundations are, for example: the making of perceptive choices among many worthy objectives; sensitivity to the strengths, the special problems, the styles of learning of the adult learner; and the development of a style for teaching which has integrity for each individual, who in turn must learn to work with his colleagues toward the integration of the whole curriculum.

But we have already begged part of the question, for by this definition we deny that subject matter enthusiasm and expertise in the teacher is self-igniting, able to provide and sustain its own thrust. Wise puts it as a question:

Does the content of Ph.D. study in a discipline provide a sufficient basis for the prospective teacher to select subject matter appropriate to the courses he will teach, and does it prepare him for the intelligent exercise of his responsibilities as a member of a college faculty which must make decisions about both purposes and procedures. . . .[21]

Burns states the issue sharply, as follows:

Even for those who obtain the doctorate, such advanced study is in most cases only a partial preparation for faculty participation. Equipped with new content, with an increased ability to manage new knowledge, with the methodology of research, the new doctor emerging from an advanced program has not of necessity had any experience or participation of education in what is involved in the organization of content for consumption by others, or in the methodology of conveying it.[22]

Nearly a generation has passed since Reynolds

. . . advanced the point of view that learning involves the whole person, and that it has important emotional and social as well as intellectual motivations. If this is true, the process of learning can only be understood in the light of all the sciences, biological, psychological and social, which are con-

---

[20] The learner in our context is an adult. It is perhaps *obiter dictum* to point out that there is a growing body of knowledge based on research which deals specifically with adult learners. The psychological foundations for use by the teacher in the education of professionals include, as well, borrowing and modifying, as necessary for his purposes, the already extensive body of "pedagogical" knowledge developed for education of the young.

[21] W. Max Wise, "Who Teaches the Teachers?" in *Improving College Teaching*, Calvin B. T. Lee, ed. (Washington: American Council on Education, 1967), p. 79.

[22] Mary E. Burns, "Advanced Curriculum and the Faculty Manpower Problem," paper presented at the CSWE Annual Program Meeting, New York, January 26, 1966, p. 5.

cerned with the dynamics of the adaptation of human beings to their physical and social world.[23]

It is a "synthesis of all these sciences" which constitutes the educational foundations for teaching.

Noting the demands set by the current curriculum policy for social work education, Witte has observed:

> But how we shall teach it, why we shall teach it in one way rather than another, and which changes we hope to bring about in those whom we are teaching in preparation for their entry into the profession—all these are questions to which the answers are far less clear. Yet they are insistent questions which must be answered if we are to teach effectively.[24]

Students who had just completed the two years of graduate study were asked in the group interview[25] to describe what in their recently completed encounter with teachers had helped and what had militated against their learning. In addition to documenting ideas about good teaching with which there is probably widespread agreement, and dividing on issues similar to those which divide many educators, the students presented some insights not likely to originate with the educators.

They took it for granted that the teacher "knew his content"—his position on the faculty of the school stipulated to this component. If he did not know specific facts, that in itself was not disconcerting. In fact, students were ready to be less demanding of a new teacher, and to bide with him in his initial floundering. True, they said, many teachers "steeped in their material" create an interest and powerful enthusiasm by their knowing, but others, equally knowledgeable, "somehow, just don't come through." Some students were upset when, with their admitted naiveté about practice, too much burden was put on them to use the theoretical material, to see the implications for practice. A few questioned the clinical wisdom of the teacher when his orientation to practice differed from the reality as the student knew it.

But most important, the students were concerned with a quality which they called "honesty" and which has different forms of expression operationally. When a basic honesty comes through, it frees the student to think and to work. He is motivated. However, as an example of what happens when this quality is absent: the teacher asks members of the class for their opinions,

---

[23] Bertha Capen Reynolds, *Learning and Teaching in the Practice of Social Work* (New York: Rinehart and Company, 1942), p. 62.

[24] Ernest F. Witte in "Foreword" to the *Teacher's Compendium*, Marguerite V. Pohek, ed. (New York: Council on Social Work Education, 1963), p. v.

[25] See abstract of group interview conducted by William Schwartz, chairman of the CSWE Faculty Development Project, in *Faculty Development in Professional Education*, Joseph Soffen, ed. (New York: Council on Social Work Education, 1967), Appendix VI, pp. 175-187.

"but you don't dare speak up, you'll be exposed"; or "when he asks for discussion but if you don't say what he expects, he cuts off the discussion." Finally, students ask: "Why do so many teachers need (seek, beg for) approval from the class? As good practitioners, they don't have the same need for approval from their clients—and they are supposed to be teaching that to us."

A good practitioner may become a good teacher, but he is not a good teacher merely by virtue of the fact that he has been a good practitioner. Although social work practice and teaching should have and do have clearly differentiated purposes and methods, certain skills are associated with all professional behavior. The transfer of skills in problem-solving or in planning, for example, is readily accomplished. That there is a generic base in the social work and the educational processes should not be minimized.

The practitioner-turned-teacher has a base available to him and he may be expected to call upon pertinent knowledge and competence he has acquired as a social worker. "In her attempts to orient educational methods to the dynamics of behavior, I believe that the social casework educator has arrived at some sound methodology."[26] (Some of us feel, in fact, that the conscientious use of this body of knowledge and experience from social work practice, transferred appropriately to educational purposes, has enriched, and can further enrich, general educational theory and practice.) The person coming to teaching with skill in social work practice has assets which he can claim for his educational role. This gives him an advantage over other prospective university professors.

Social workers turned educators know deep "in their bones" the *importance* of the professional relationship which fuels the process in social work helping. They also know *how to use* the relationship between the professional self and the client. They will therefore recognize the same concept, as it has been developed for the educational process, as useful:

> Just as we have had to shift our understanding of the learning process from the process to the learner, so we are now discovering the understanding of teaching is not to be found in methods but in the teacher. The teacher is first and foremost a person, a self. He is not a library, not a machine, not a disseminator of knowledge. He is a human being interacting with other human beings in a very human process. Learning to teach is not a question of learning to *do* something; it is a matter of learning to *be* something.[27]

Although referring to the professional social worker, Schwartz has given precision to the concept of interaction and relationship which is also applicable in the learning process:

[26] Towle, *op. cit.*, p. xvii.

[27] Arthur W. Combs, "Teachers Too Are Individuals," *The Self in Growth, Teaching and Learning*, Don E. Hamachek, ed. (Englewood Cliffs, N. J.: Prentice-Hall, 1965), p. 458.

From our experience we can testify that there are "knowers," who cannot help anybody, and there are "feelers," who cannot put their feelings to use in the service of people. Ultimately, both cognition and affect must be transmuted into ways of listening and responding, and it is these operations, consistently reproduced, that represent the educational payoff in any profession.[28]

Looking back on more than three decades of teaching, Wessel contemplates "a very old and familiar conflict of values in which the teacher becomes entangled."

It is the controversy over the relative value of man's two inescapable motives —the practical and the contemplative. Which is more noble—to do or to think? . . . to act (to teach) or to contemplate (to search for and discover new knowledge).

For herself, she concludes:

Those of us who teach where both motives are thus valued, who are privileged to work in this "perfection of unity" are blessed, indeed . . .

I can tell you that it is purest joy to feel yourself kindling into being the students' intellectual interests, liberating their minds to become engaged in new discovery of themselves and their world; and liberating their feelings, towards finding fresh and deeper insights.

It is also pure aesthetic pleasure to feel yourself, each time, re-creating and re-inventing the whole process and content, the whole drama, in teaching a class, no matter how many times you have taught the course before.[29]

We have not differentiated, in this discussion of the need for ability to teach, between classroom and field teachers. Their methodologies vary, as has been clarified by Towle and Schwartz.[30] However, the field instructor must also have preparation for his teaching function.

The shift from practitioner to educator is a complex one. . . . Training must prepare him to perform this new role competently. The field instructor must have a thorough understanding of available educational concepts regarding learning patterns and teaching methods and of ways to interrelate the two; . . . in learning to use his knowledge of personality dynamics and

---

[28] William Schwartz, "The Classroom Teaching of Social Work with Groups: Some Central Problems," A Conceptual Framework for the Teaching of the Social Group Work Method in the Classroom (New York: Council on Social Work Education, 1964), p. 6.

[29] Rosa Wessel, "Response," on receiving award on the occasion of her retirement, April 29, 1966. (Mimeographed.)

[30] Charlotte Towle, The Case Method in Teaching Social Work (New York: National Association of Social Workers, 1959). That field teaching has a distinct function which has its own effective methodology is further explicated by William Schwartz, op. cit. The methodology of field instruction is increasingly being studied in a systematic manner. See, Field Instruction in Graduate Social Work Education—Old Problems and New Proposals (New York: Council on Social Work Education, 1966).

treatment procedures in order to make educational diagnoses and teaching plans.[31]

An educational enterprise is derelict if it does not develop standards for good teaching that can be recognized and valued. One can learn how to teach, and an intuitively good teacher can become a better one. There is a growing body of educational knowledge—philosophy, psychology, and "know-how"—available to those who would exploit it. To ignore it is to short-change the profession. True, some master teachers never had an "education course," many teachers are good teachers with only native qualities, and many have learned to be good teachers out of their own firing-line experience. (This line of reasoning might also be used to denigrate the importance of education for professional practice: all professions value the "natural"—the intuitive individual—grant that experience too is a teacher, and still require the same formal credentials from all.[32]) We cannot settle for anything less than the best for increasing, improving, and maximally using the scarce and valued social work educator.

> The nature and quality of college teaching directly affect the educative or miseducative quality of the student's experience. The nature of the learning opportunity can be as potent a factor as the substantive being studied.[33]

Summary

Four components of preparation have been specified. Additional questions have also been asked: How much of each component and for whom? To ask these questions obviously suggests that all faculty cannot and should not be expected to be equally prepared in all areas of content, be equally steeped in practice wisdom or skill, be equally active in research. Just as there must be specialization of content, so is it appropriate to recognize gradations and specialization within the practice and research components.

There are many gradations of the practice component, ranging from a basic orientation which is quite different from deep skill and practice wisdom. Similarly, many levels of research, understanding, and skill can be identified, from research-mindedness—valuing research and knowing how to use research findings in teaching—to ability to participate in sophisticated research activities, and finally, imaginative and initiating research skill. All members of a faculty need a basic level of research-mindedness if they are to fulfill the expecta-

---

[31] Aleanor Merrifield, "Changing Patterns and Programs in Field Instruction," *Social Service Review*, Vol. 37, No. 31 (September, 1963), p. 278.

[32] Pohek recalls that "this dialogue rings a familiar bell. Is it not strangely reminiscent of the early days of casework, when fear was . . . expressed lest natural skill in relationship be submerged in concern with . . . method and the art of helping be lost in scientific technique?" See Marguerite V. Pohek, "Toward a Methodology of Teaching," in *Education for Social Work* (New York: Council on Social Work Education, 1964), p. 154.

[33] Florence B. Stratemeyer, *op. cit.*, p. 38.

51

tions set for them by the curriculum. Some must be able to initiate and to teach research. Research skill is no more an absolute quality than are any of the other components.

The faculty member must be a generalist in the sense that he qualifies, at least at a basic level, both in practice and in research. Granted that there will be special instances—as distinct from the general criteria—such as the social scientist whose contribution to the curriculum has its own rationale. All should be specialists in an area of curriculum content, as well as in either practice or research. (Specialists in both practice and research just don't come very often!) But all must have the ability to teach.

The needs of the field, the mission of the university and of its professional schools, and the "given" inherent in the nature of faculty—the human component—each of these stipulates difference. The arena for social welfare activities was never unitary; today its complexity is staggering, and the outlines of its future are not fully known. Objectives and emphases are ordered differently from university to university and from school to school, as they should continue to be. The "human condition" of difference is a strength as well as a necessity. In short, it seems wise to avoid aiming either for the "model teacher" or the "model faculty." Each faculty will usefully have its own face. As Perlman has teasingly noted, a faculty can be "oddly assorted" or "richly diverse."

TO LEARN TO TEACH: A CHALLENGE TO SOCIAL WORK EDUCATION

by Lila Swell*

The quality and direction of social work education, and, indeed, of education itself, are undergoing some critical re-thinking. The impetus behind the search for new methods and goals lies within a complex social and technological revolution, every bit as far-reaching in its implications as the industrial revolution was a century ago. In seriously thinking about what to teach and how to teach it, issues which are themselves complex and controversial, social work educators must and are beginning to consider the question of preparation of the new teacher. What type of foundation is necessary for the new teacher if he is to meet the challenge of classroom teaching with originality, creativeness, and effectiveness?

In the following discussion, a possible approach to the pre-service preparation of social work educators is put forward. A theoretical framework for teacher training is considered, and two possible methods for actualizing this program are proposed: first, in a combined social work and education doctoral program, and second, through an in-service training program in schools of social work. Some thought is also given to the rationale for having such programs at all. Why must we prepare teachers to teach?

Teacher training is a subject of rather recent interest. In retracing the history of our current dialogue on preparing social work educators one may feel a bit like Old Mother Hubbard. The cupboard is not bare, but the shelf labeled "Thoughts on Teacher Preparation" is only beginning to be stocked with goods. There are reasons for this. Throughout recorded time, men have learned and men have taught. No one taught Socrates how to teach. The prerequisite for teaching was knowledge; effective transmission of this knowledge depended upon the artistry and intuition of the teacher and the tenacity of the learner. Education as a distinct field, and teaching as a specific profession, have come into their own only in this century.

* This paper is an expansion of a discussion presented at the CSWE Sixteenth Annual Program Meeting, Minneapolis, Minnesota, January, 1968. At that time Dr. Swell was assistant professor of casework at the School of Social Service Administration, University of Chicago. She is currently serving as Educational Consultant at the W. Clement and Jessie V. Stone Foundation.

To be sure, art and intuition are important aspects of teaching. But with the elevation of teaching to the status of profession has come the development of a rapidly expanding, codifiable, transmittable body of knowledge. It is a body of knowledge concerned with the process of teaching and learning itself. It is a body of knowledge which supplements intuition with theory and method. It does not deny that there is such a thing as the naturally gifted teacher. It does say that in teaching, as in social work practice, even the "natural" can and does benefit from training.

The question to which we in social work must address ourselves therefore is: how and to what extent must we make this knowledge viable and available? Considering the present level of development of educational theories, it is archaic and wasteful to proceed on the premise that each new teacher must learn his profession and develop his art mainly through trial and error.

This point seems obvious and yet it is often ignored. Teaching is a profession. The social worker who goes into education is entering a second profession—teaching. He should be equally prepared in the dual role of social worker/teacher. For years we have been vitally concerned with qualifications and standards for practitioners. We are only now beginning to recognize that the teacher should be as well-prepared to teach as the practitioner is to practice!

The new teacher must cross a bridge from practice and the field to the classroom. To be structurally sound, the blocks of this bridge must be built of both theoretical and practical knowledge. The program I am presenting here would transmit this knowledge through course work in five areas: (1) content, (2) learning theory, (3) teaching methodology, (4) group process and leadership techniques, and (5) curriculum development. In addition to didactic work in these five areas, the program includes a structured teaching internship.

The first phase of teacher preparation is the area of *content*. Prior to entering a training program, the teacher-to-be must have demonstrated a high degree of mastery of the knowledge and skills of his particular area of practice. He must have not only sufficient skill in or talent for direct practice but sufficient mastery of content and ability to conceptualize that content as well. This degree of professional maturity would probably require, ideally, *at least* five years of experience in the field. The settings and quality of that experience should also be considered.

Beyond these, there is still a difference in the degree and quality of conceptualization demanded in teaching as opposed to the field. The teacher must be able not only to conceptualize, with respect to a particular case, but also to formulate clearly and convey generalized principles of social work practice. This task is likely to be even more difficult if the new teacher has not had experience in field instruction, which more and more demands the teaching of both principles and concepts. Furthermore, a university or college faculty member in social work is increasingly expected to have a broad range of knowledge of the social sciences as well as of research. This necessitates advanced study, particularly in the new teacher's area of expertise.

The content segment of any teacher training program should not be construed to imply only advanced study of content new to the teacher. Equally strong emphasis should be given to the *content of the master's program in which he is to teach.* The new teacher must struggle to conceptualize and reconceptualize principles of social work which have become so well-integrated for him as to be reflexive. But he has yet a further task: these concepts must be translated to the level of the student. The new teacher must, to paraphrase an axiom of casework, learn to start where the student is. And he has to know where the student should be at the end of a semester, a year, two years.

Learning theory, the second area of formal education, is closely intertwined with content. In order to convey content effectively and be able to teach with efficacy, one should understand how and under what conditions people learn. The psychology of learning for the educator is no abstract stimulus-response configuration, but includes the most practical and useful concepts about how learning occurs, such as: the role of motivation in learning; progression in learning, i.e., timing—the fact that learning proceeds from the known to the unknown and from the simple to the complex; repetition in various forms enhances learning; and partialization is necessary for learning to occur.

Teaching methodology, the third area of formal education, also deals with content—precisely, the question of how to present content in such a way as to maximize learning. Educational methodologists, within as well as outside of social work, have produced a wealth of thoughtful and thought-provoking material on how to use case records, films, role-playing, audio and videotapes, lectures, discussions, and panels in the classroom. These teaching methodologists are increasingly expanding their awareness and utilization of the fruits of the new educational technology, i.e., programmed learning, computerized instruction, and so on.

Teacher training includes the rationale and the means of implementing these methods. The new teacher, fortified with knowledge of content, often feels quite helpless and at sea in communicating this knowledge. Teaching methodology gives the new teacher the tools he needs to convey knowledge. More than that, it gives him an understanding of *how knowledge is conveyed.* He already knows, for instance, that he must identify principles. Teaching methodology tells him *how.* He learns how various methods can be used to relay the concepts and principles he wants to teach. In this way, teaching methodology becomes not a matter of style but rather a matter of disciplined technique, analogous to specific treatment techniques employed to attain a therapeutic goal.

The fourth area of preceptive training for the new teacher is in *group process and leadership techniques.* Group process and leadership techniques are related to the psychology of learning as mentioned above. They are also related to, and could be considered a part of, teaching methodology. We know, for instance, that there is such a thing as resistance to learning. Educational group leadership techniques provide knowledge of how to cope with the resistive learner, for example.

This is not to say that the teacher is a "classical" group leader. He is not. His role is much more that of a conveyor of knowledge and a facilitator of learning. Nonetheless, when situations do arise in a class which threaten the equilibrium of the class and thus the goals of the educational group, the teacher should have some idea of how to handle the situation. The difficulty in role transition from helper to teacher comes to the fore when problems such as resistance arise in the learning group. The new teacher must learn to maintain his role of instructor while drawing upon his knowledge of human behavior in order to become an enabler in the learning process. This may be particularly difficult for the new teacher who has had little or no experience with groups of learners.

Although his role is different from that of practitioner, much of his knowledge about enabling is carried over from practice experience. For instance, resistance must be dealt with openly when it affects the entire group, just as it must be aired openly with a client or clients. Another principle carried over from the field is that students, like clients, must feel acceptance, encouragement, and freedom of expression in order to realize their potential for growth. The task of the new teacher is to apply principles of practice common to the class without confusing his and the student's own role. The teacher is only a helper in the learning process, not a therapist.

The study of small group process has much to say about how learning groups are formed and the process of growth and change which they undergo. Group leadership techniques, as applied to learning groups, provide a framework for handling common day-to-day class situations, including creation of a positive atmosphere for learning and working effectively with non-verbal class members, hostile members, exceptionally bright students, students with good prior experience, competitiveness in the classroom, and so on.

The fifth area of didactic education for the new teacher is in *curriculum development*. Curriculum development is based on expertise in content and the use of learning theory in determining the timing of the presentation of that content. It deals with course objectives and the educational steps toward attaining these goals. As stated in the 1960 Report of the National Curriculum Workshop of the Council on Social Work Education:

> The purpose of curriculum organization is to maximize the cumulative effect of all the learning experiences.

> The principles of *continuity, sequence,* and *integration* are useful in planning this organization:

Continuity in the curriculum involves continuing emphasis over a period of time on the major aspects of behavior the student is to learn. . . .

Sequence in the curriculum involves planning so that each learning experience will add something new in order to build on previous experiences, but to go beyond them. . . .

Curriculum arrangements which are made to aid students in integrating their learning are referred to as *integration* of the curriculum. The faculty, recognizing the specialized responsibility of discrete courses, need to put these courses in some pattern that will bring about effective integration by the student.[1]

The same principles of clarifying objectives and organizing curriculum apply equally to the total program of the school, the development of a sequence, and a particular course. Each course has specific objectives with regard to the content to be taught. For example, one *objective* of a casework course might be to teach psychosocial diagnosis. Thus the content is determined by the objectives of the course. In addition to being able to set clear goals for his own course, the new teacher must have some familiarity with the total curriculum. This is necessary for understanding the role of his particular course within the gestalt of the professional school. He must also understand that the curriculum changes as new trends emerge in life and practice.

The five areas briefly mentioned above would make up the formal or pedagogical portion of the teacher-training model. Of equal importance in the preparation of new teachers is practice in teaching—the experience referred to here as a teaching internship. The internship is multifaceted. It should not be used as a trial or testing period, but rather a learning period. It involves classroom teaching and the evaluation of that teaching through various devices such as individual consultation with a senior faculty member, participant-observer, direct observation of class sessions, co-teaching, review of tapes of class sessions, and meetings with other interns to share experiences. The advent of videotape offers yet another means of doing this though microteaching, which permits the teacher to observe his own performance on videotape and to receive evaluations from his peers.

Regular and careful consultation is an important aid to the new teacher. The difference, however, between consultation and supervision must be strongly emphasized. In consultation there is a give and take. The new faculty member brings his freshness of practice experience and the senior member brings his richness of teaching experience. The traditional idea of social work supervision is foreign and alien to academic tradition. If consultation is im-

---

[1] *Building the Social Work Curriculum* (New York: Council on Social Work Education, 1960), p. 51.

portant for the new teacher, freedom is equally important. The new teacher must feel free to create and use *himself* effectively. He must feel free to experiment, try new approach models, adapt techniques to suit his own emerging style. In a teacher preparation program, the balance between structure and freedom may be difficult to attain. The goal, nonetheless, must be to train with thoroughness but without rigidity, to inform without forcing the teacher to conform.

A free, consultative relationship with senior faculty members is therefore essential if new faculty members are to develop as creative and effective teachers. The supervisory relationship is based on evaluation and power whereas the consultative relationship is based on information and competence. Individuals are expected to work as a cohesive unit, each having something to offer. The results are antithetical to those of a power system where senior members become strong at the expense of subordinates, who tend to become weak and ineffectual. Mediocrity is often rewarded in a pyramidal system, for the creative individual might rock the boat, and such a system cannot tolerate waves. The effects of a supervisory system on an individual and on an organization have been described by Dr. Chris Argyris, chairman of the Department of Administrative Sciences at Yale, who found:

> Weak subordinates, in turn, protected themselves from the strong superior by carefully censoring the information they sent to the superior, or "timing" the moment he would receive it. . . . As a result, dry runs became a way of life; timing became even more valued than thinking; fighting and polarizing issues more rewarded than open cooperation and problem-solving. All these consequences tended to make organizations increasingly rigid and sticky. . . . In a world where power is used as a major force to get compliance [and conformity], it is usually accompanied by the use of guilt and exhortation. ("If you do not do what I ask you, you are bad and therefore I must punish you.") The basis for loyalty is fear and guilt.[2]

Carl Rogers spoke of the same thing from a different frame of reference when he said, "When we cease to form judgments of the other individual from our own locus of evaluation, we are fostering creativity. . . . Evaluation is always a threat, always creates a need for defensiveness, always means that some portion of experience must be denied to awareness . . . to cease evaluating is not to cease having reactions. It may, as a matter of fact, free one to react."[3]

Creative teaching cannot occur in an atmosphere where new approaches and differences are felt to be dangerous, or where new ideas are "judged" rather than "reacted to." If the new teacher is not free to create and innovate,

---

[2] Chris Argyris, "How Tomorrow's Executives Will Make Decisions," *Think*, Vol. 33, No. 6 (November-December, 1967), pp. 21-22.

[3] Carl Rogers, "Toward a Theory of Creativity," *Etc.*, A *Review of General Semantics*, Vol. XI, No. 4 (Summer, 1954), p. 257.

then his talent cannot be fully used, the system itself will become increasingly nonviable and, most important, the student will suffer. Long ago, John Dewey espoused the principle that teaching should be student-centered, not subject-centered. If the student's potential is to be fully developed, the teacher must be able to encourage creativity—an impossible task if the teacher is not permitted to be, or cannot allow himself to be, creative. The goals and methods of pre-service preparation of new faculty directly affect the students. This process has been succinctly described by Frank Williams, who says:

> Studies have shown that a consistent effort to use the wide range of mental processes at least latent in most students requires of the teacher much conscious effort, knowledge of the widely varied and less familiar modes of thinking, and many new teaching styles. . . . Teachers must be shown how subject matter can be presented at various conceptual levels in ways which encourage the students to aspire to novelty, to develop fluidity of associations, to possess flexibility in thinking patterns, and to probe new dimensions of knowledge. Student intellectual creativity demands both ample opportunity for its exercise and challenging instruction—in a classroom atmosphere of encouragement and approval for such endeavor. Teachers themselves must also be given freedom to construct and experiment. . . .[4]

This point is given particular emphasis because, presumably, the ultimate goal of any teacher-training program is better education for the students. On the path towards this goal, an atmosphere conducive to optimum teaching is necessary for optimum learning. The way in which a new teacher is trained must include attitudes as well as mechanics.

At the present time the need for trained social work practitioners is escalating rapidly, and there is great pressure on existing schools to expand and for new schools to be established. The need for trained faculty members is therefore all the more urgent and the need for a practical induction and training program all the more critical. The most *comprehensive vehicle* for this training could be the establishment of a graduate program leading to a Doctor of Education in Social Work degree. Schools of social work increasingly desire that new faculty members have a doctorate. While the Ph.D. remains unparalleled in academic excellence and esteem, as currently constituted it is neither fish nor fowl in terms of preparing candidates to teach. The present orientation, as is well known, is likely to be towards research rather than teaching. The orientation of the proposed Doctor of Education in Social Work degree would be primarily towards training social work educators. In addition to the five major areas of study outlined above, such a doctoral program could include the internship, more advanced study of the social sciences, and a dissertation based on a teaching project.

It is hard to escape the logic of an advanced degree program which teaches

---

[4] Frank E. Williams, "Intellectual Creativity and the Teacher," *The Journal of Creative Behavior*, Vol. 1, No. 2 (Spring, 1967), p. 179.

teachers how to teach. Increasingly over the past seven years, schools in the fields of law, medicine, history, biology, and on down the line have concerned themselves with the problem of teaching teachers how to teach. It is even more essential that such consideration be given in social work education since learning involves content which is anxiety-laden for the student. Emotionally laden content evokes resistance to learning. Thus, the teacher must know something about progression in learning, how people learn, blocks to learning, and supportive approaches when anxiety is high. An additional burden for the student of social work, besides the fact that his own feelings and conflicts are aroused, is that his becoming a professional social worker necessitates attitudinal change and development. Intellectual mastery of a body of knowledge may suffice in biology but is not enough in social work. The additional demands of social work learning, I feel, require greater skill in social work teaching. On a practical level, such a program of training teachers of social work could be operated cooperatively by a school of social work and a school of education.

The above program would not in itself provide the total answer to the problem of recruiting and preparing social work educators. As Eileen Blackey pointed out in 1964, "It is unrealistic to think that [the then][5] 61 schools of social work in the United States can expect to fill faculty ranks from graduates of doctoral programs, even if everyone in such programs elected teaching as a career choice."[6] This reality behooves us to question whether and how a rigorous program for teacher preparation, such as outlined here, might be modified or adapted to in-service training. This is more than a question of practicalities. The doctoral candidate is expected only to *learn* whereas the new faculty member requiring in-service teacher training has a *job* to do regardless of his own learning requirements. This can lead to a conflict in values and necessitates the setting of priorities. The new faculty member cannot be a teacher, learner, committee member, field liaison, student advisor, writer, and community leader simultaneously in his first year. Each of these roles, with slight variation among different schools, is an important aspect of professorial functioning as a social work educator. Given that the member of a faculty eventually must feel comfortable in many cloaks—which should he try on and be fitted for first? We are agreed that priorities must be set in order to avoid splintering the time of new faculty members. In the long run it is worth our while to assign primary value to knowledge of content and teaching skills.

If teaching were given first priority, a rigorous training model could be

---

[5] The number has now risen to 71, as listed by the Council on Social Work Education in July, 1968.

[6] Eileen Blackey, "Issues in Social Work Education—New and Changing Demands Made of the Profession," *Proceedings, Education for Social Work*, No. 12, 1964, p. 83.

adapted to fit an in-service mode. The first year of employment for a new faculty member might consist of a structured and balanced program leading to a certificate in social work education. One way such a program might be effected would be to hire the new teacher in June and begin with a summer of course work (such as content, learning theory, and teaching methodology). This would enable the teacher to have some formal preparation before facing his first class. The first year of teaching would be handled like the internship, discussed before. In addition to actual teaching, the internship includes seminars with other interns where tapes of class sessions would be reviewed as to content and method. General problems of teaching and identification of principles to be taught in cases would be discussed in a group or in individual consultation with a senior faculty member. Demands on faculty in their first year for committee work, advising, and so on should be limited. The new teacher could get some familiarity with all aspects of his job and still concentrate on one—teaching. A second summer—or part of a summer—could be used to complete didactic education leading to the certificate in social work education.

The foregoing discussion has centered around several major themes. First, the importance of teaching as a profession. Second, the need for the teacher, as a professional, to familiarize himself with a certain body of knowledge, five aspects of which were discussed. Third, two educational tracks which could be used to make this knowledge available to new social work educators. These two tracks need not be mutually exclusive; in fact, one complements the other. Even the teacher who has received a doctorate or advanced training in social work education can benefit from on-going education for teachers. The situation is comparable to that of the practitioner who, as a professional, must keep up with the literature, new trends in education, etc.

Creative thinking about teacher education is crucial if social work education is ever to provide the quality and number of teachers the field of social work demands. The framework of training presented today airs two possible methods of preparing new teachers. This framework represents one approach —not the only answer to the problem. The great need for trained teachers presents a challenge to all schools of social work not to coast along but to innovate; not to rest on the laurels of present programs but to re-evaluate; not to settle for the minimum but to strive for the maximum. Although we still have a long way to go, we have made a start. The current concern of the Council on Social Work Education and the thinking and planning going on in many of our graduate schools testify to this fact. There are many ways to get to Rome and we are just beginning to build new roads.

Part II

On Becoming a Teacher:
The Induction Period

ON BECOMING A TEACHER:
THE INDUCTION PERIOD

New faculty bring a range of strengths and differential needs. They have come by a way of several routes: the professional, the academic, or the acculturation routes. However, together they all face induction into a new career in a professional school within a complex university system. The induction period has its own demands and creates fairly universal needs, associated with the transition itself. They include socialization to the university, to the school of social work, and to the field of social work education. There are needs arising from role diversity and role ambiguity in university life, and, of course, there are expectations for effective teaching.

A large proportion of new faculty come from positions in social work practice where their competence was unquestioned. In fact, they were selected because of their status or recognized performance. They come to positions which have major and immediate expectations set for them, or which they feel have been set for them, with less than complete conviction about their adequacy for meeting these expectations. These problems are on a level different from the anxieties attendant upon any change from one job setting to another. They are associated with the expectations set for a university professor. Some of these expectations are self-imposed; some are imposed by the institution and its administrators; some by colleagues in the school of social work or in other departments of the university. Students also set expectations for faculty. Many know little about the totality of social work education—the field, its interrelationships, and its resources.

There are differences between social agency and university cultures. A major contrast is to be found in the valued tradition within the university of *academic freedom* on the one hand, and of *professional responsibility* in social agency practice on the other. The duty and the right of the scholar to teach the truth as he sees it, and to challenge ancient truths are inviolable; they are rights that have been won and re-won in each generation and must continually be guarded against infringements. Structures which suggest administrative hierarchy are avoided. On the other hand, accountability of the social worker to society on behalf of the agency's clients is carefully provided for through a supervisory structure within each agency, that gives it a quality in sharp contrast to the traditional climate of a university.

With reference to role diversity and role ambiguity, a new faculty member knows that he is expected to carry new roles but the roles are not clear. He has an idealized image of the scholar role but has no experience with it. There is also a new "colleague role" with professors from other departments of the university. The role as liaison between school and agency, such as in-the-field advising, is a new one. He finds different expectations for different faculty; he senses different expectations in a professional school from those in the traditional academic departments.

A useful conceptualization of the distinctive demands for role clarity made by the university is offered by Blau, who points out several characteristics that distinguish universities from other complex organizations. For example, the relationship betwen staff and line is reversed in the university: administrative authority and professional staff relationships are more difficult to show in a hierarchical arrangement than in most other bureaucracies. Second, "whereas most formal organizations tend to draw clear boundaries between the members of the organization and its public, this is not true of the universities." Most intriguing is the characteristic of universities, which:

> . . . are institutional arrangements for regular production of two ingredients of social change. The first is original ideas and the second is men to implement these ideas and produce others. . . . Universities have the functions of developing both new ideas and the producers of new ideas; merely communicating the most recent results of research and training men to apply them could be done in separate institutions.[1]

There is considerable recognition and response to the needs indigenous to the induction period. An inventory of reported induction activities and experiences is impressive. New faculty often refer to the fortuitous availability of a more experienced colleague. Some recall a sense of isolation in a "sink or swim" atmosphere. Others report that they found planned conferences with the dean or with a senior faculty member, either on a regular or "as needed" basis, to be useful.

Many schools rely upon the dynamics of the informal but powerful system which operates in a faculty. There is considerable agreement about the need for explicating the institutional and professional expectations while retaining and maximally exploiting the values of the colleagual, i.e., informal system.

The selections in this part have been chosen to stimulate discussion and exploration by groups of new faculty early in their induction period, whether these groupings are formal, under the guidance of an assigned mentor, or are spontaneously organized. Or, they may serve as a source of reinforcement for the new faculty member as he seeks on his own to make the transition a positive one.

New faculty may find a fraternal bond with the anonymous author whose "Random Thoughts" appear first. They may also sense a community of interest in the problems and discussion in the selections that follow.

---

[1] Peter M. Blau, "The University as a Distinctive Organization," in *Institutional Backgrounds of Adult Education*, R. J. Ingham, ed. (Boston: Center for the Study of Liberal Education for Adults at Boston University, 1966), p. 98. See also, Logan Wilson, "The Professor and His Roles," in *Improving College Teaching*, Calvin Lee, ed. (Washington: American Council on Education, 1967), pp. 99-109.

RANDOM THOUGHTS OF A
NEW FACULTY MEMBER

Anonymous

I think it is assumed that the new faculty member in the lower ranks has more need for orientation to his role as a member of the faculty than those in higher ranks. This may be the assumption and expectation of those of lower rank. Nevertheless, there is danger that new faculty of lower rank may have to assume considerable responsibility for the problems of higher education today. There was a time when a school's acquiring a new staff member must have been a joy. Now to get a new staff member is considered by the faculty to be a burden, as he is one more individual who has to be trained. New faculty becomes a part of the problem and not a solution to the problem. Consequently, I believe the new faculty person must assume great responsibility for his own orientation.

The first problem the new faculty person faces is that of defining the components of his new position. The description of tasks or workload of the new faculty member offers some clue as to the nature and number of the component parts of his new position. He teaches so many courses which meet once each week for a term; he advises X number of students who are placed at specific field work sites. Teaching and advisement then are two important components of the new position. However, if he is to identify with the total task of professional education, he becomes concerned about his role as a member of a faculty which has responsibility for educational policy-making. More important, he has responsibility for implementing segments of the school's program as well as integrating his teaching and advisement function into the total program. If he is a faculty field instructor, field teaching is another segment of the workload.

I have defined for myself components of the job of a "junior faculty" member. However, with schools expanding so rapidly at the present time, "senior faculty" may also be new. In order to determine the areas in which the new person seeks orientation, I enumerate the following components:

1. *Teaching.* How do I know what students already know? What are the creative uses of the small group for learning? How do I select facts and theory to be presented? How do I make creative use of the assignment? I recall learning through intellectual assignments that were challenging and stimu-

lating, but I find it hard to make challenging and stimulating assignments. I experience "being relevant" as a real problem each time I meet a class.

2. *Advisement.*   How much do I need to know about what is going on for a student in his field work experience? What does my school think the role of the field advisor is?

3. *Faculty Member.*   I want to know more about the history and philosophy of higher education. What is the nature of the organization of the university and what in the organization promotes and deters learning? I should like to have an organizational chart of the total university. Who gives the right to the new faculty member to identify with the organization; is it one's colleagues or is it the administration?

What are the criteria for determining curriculum appropriate to higher education? Many new faculty members have thought about this matter long before coming to a graduate school to teach, but the problem for the new faculty member is to determine not only what his colleagues say they think about these things but also to learn about how the school practices what it says it believes.

Perhaps any induction program needs to make explicit what can be accomplished through formal and informal structures of the university organization. The informal structures in most organizations are powerful forces in induction and may be most enabling or almost paralyzing in their influence. Some substantive as well as adaptative element of a new faculty's preparation may be provided through the informal structure. As for myself, for the substantive, my mind and soul long for the Ph.D.; for the adaptative—a few rounds with an analyst and the friendship and goodwill of my colleagues.

A burden felt by many new faculty stems from the dilemma of being "untrained educators." Whether with or without doctorates, they feel that whatever they have to offer is not enough.

ORIENTATION OF NEW FACULTY

by Victoria Olds *

(Among the recommendations made to the CSWE by the Faculty Development Project were two which urged the CSWE "to undertake responsibility for a major comprehensive and planned recruitment effort to inform, interest, and attract potential faculty," and also "to undertake responsibility for participating with the schools in programs designed to assist new faculty in their transition during the induction phase."

As a response to these recommendations, and with the aid of a grant from NIMH, the CSWE has expanded its program in relation to recruitment and development of new faculty. In this paper, Dr. Olds, from her vantage point of staff member in the expanded program, reports to new full-time faculty members, to those who would like to be educators, and to the senior faculty members who have an interest in or responsibility for the orientation of new faculty members. Ed.)

NEEDS AND PRACTICES

As one way of learning about the needs of new faculty as viewed from their own perspectives, a questionnaire was sent in October, 1967, to 276 new faculty members in the 69 schools that had filed reports about faculty additions with the CSWE.

The questions asked of the new faculty were the following:

1. What steps did you find most helpful to you in your induction as a faculty member?
2. What suggestions do you have for other steps which might have facilitated your induction and preparation for teaching?
3. What recommendations would you make for an orderly preparation for new faculty both prior to the beginning of classes or field, and during the first year of teaching, whether in class or field?
4. In what ways do you think the Council can be of help to you and to other prospective new faculty members?

Responses came from 77 new faculty members of 43 schools, or 28% of the total group who were sent questionnaires. The 43 schools represented 62% of the 69 schools involved. The responses were thoughtful appraisals of the

* Excerpts from a paper presented at the CSWE Sixteenth Annual Program Meeting, January 25, 1968, in Minneapolis, Minnesota. At that time Dr. Olds was CSWE Consultant on Recruitment and Development of New Faculty.

current patterns used in the orientation of new faculty. The comments which follow are not intended to be a rigorous analysis of faculty reaction. They are revealing as a sampling of the thinking of new faculty in relation to their own orientation experiences.

The responses to the first question included a wide range of specific activities related to orientation. In several instances the new faculty member reported that he had had no orientation at all and was thrust immediately into a job assignment. The patterns of orientation of new faculty were as varied as the number of schools represented. Each school had its own pattern and its own rationale for its program. In analyzing the responses, it became apparent that despite the variations there were many similarities. These can be loosely classified in terms of *when, where, what, how,* and *with whom* the orientation process was carried out.

With regard to the matter of *when,* the timing of the orientation was seen as important. A request made repeatedly was for more time so that the new person could learn some fundamentals about the various areas involved before he was put under pressure of meeting demands from students. New faculty expressed great appreciation when time was allowed for pre-service preparation, i.e., prior to the date of assumption of job responsibilities. Practice varied from no time to a full semester or a summer of orientation. Many schools followed a pattern of several days' retreat prior to the opening of school. The emphasis on the need for more time in which to prepare was also reflected in a request for a light teaching load during the first year because of the time needed to fill the knowledge gaps in several areas. Several responses indicated that it takes more time the first year to prepare a course outline as compared with the time required to prepare modifications of that course in subsequent years.

The orientation with regard to *where* was also a matter of concern. The concept of *place* was extended to include not only having one's own desk, and an office; learning the facilities of the school, of the campus, of the community; and learning the agencies in which field work instruction was based; but also having secretarial help, knowing where the library was, and having adequate library resources for one's own learning as well as for planning student assignments.

The *what* of the content of orientation was complex and required a careful sorting out of what information was needed immediately and what could be referred to in passing, with the understanding that there would be a follow-up at a later point. In some ways the content of orientation can be compared to a formal curriculum inasmuch as some components are more advanced and required prerequisites of knowledge and experience. In general, the new faculty wanted to start with the immediate and the concrete, such as beginning with an individual course and moving to the sequence and then to the overall curriculum. There were some differences in the responses of

70

those new faculty who came to teaching after completion of their own doctoral study. These new teachers felt more prepared because their knowledge gap was not too great. They were inclined to see their needs more in the area of how to teach and how to manage a classroom than in the area of substantive knowledge content. They wanted more advanced discussions of educational theory and practice.

The job aspects of being a new faculty member were important. Mention was made of the need to know specifically about the conditions of employment, the fringe benefits accruing to a faculty member, the routes to professional development, to achievement of tenure, to promotion in rank.

In terms of the *who* in orientation, the responses revealed an interest in having a specific senior faculty member designated as responsible for the orientation process even though segments of the orientation program could be assigned to other faculty. Some interest was also expressed for a preceptor or mentor who could serve not so much as a supervisor, but rather as a counselor, a friendly critic to whom the new faculty could freely go with a wide variety of questions. This senior faculty person might possibly be someone in the same sequence who could help also in the planning and construction of the course, and in the discussion of teaching methods. Another need expressed was a wish for discussion meetings with peers, with only other new faculty as a separate group, and with total faculty, as in general faculty meetings. With peers who were newcomers, it would be possible to discuss common problems of newness. The general faculty meetings were seen as essential to new faculty as a source of information about the total school program, and about problems facing all faculty.

The *how* of the orientation could assume many shapes. Personal contact was given high priority—in individual conferences with the dean, with the coordinator of curriculum, with the director of field work, or with the sequence chairman. These were all seen as most helpful. Didactic instruction in the form of lectures was found helpful, because of the tremendous knowledge gap usually faced by new faculty members. A wish was expressed for written materials, such as faculty handbooks which would contain general information about the total university as well as the school of social work. Course syllabi, bibliographies, and other curriculum materials were seen as highly desirable.

Meetings with students in the regular student orientation program were seen as useful. One variation of this was to assign to new faculty some responsibility for the orientation of new students. In this way, the new faculty enhanced their own orientation learning by helping to orient students.

Other resources included observational experiences such as having new faculty audit courses and attend seminars. There was little evidence that senior faculty as master teachers were called upon to give demonstration classes for observation by the new faculty. There were a few instances of planned formal educational experiences for new faculty, such as seminars in educational theory and methodology. One of the drawbacks noted was that the workloads of senior faculty members were not adjusted so that they could give the necessary attention to the orientation and development of new faculty. In several instances, the new faculty commented that they hesitated to make demands on the senior faculty because they were too preoccupied and under pressure. Much learning apparently was derived from informal unplanned contacts with faculty. These contacts were reported as occurring on an ad hoc basis and usually on the initiative of the new faculty members.

Faculty field instructors noted that there was a demand on them to operate within two social systems, agency and school, and to achieve a useful bridging of theory and practice. The teaching within the agency was to be guided by the school's curriculum and yet was to remain consistent with the agency's expectations and requirements. Some of the faculty field teachers reported that it was difficult to develop a comfortable identification as a member of a school faculty when most of the working hours were spent in the agency. They felt their task was more arduous than that of the classroom teacher.

In a list of helpful steps which were suggested by the respondents, mention must be made of a request for a kit which they wanted to have prior to the opening of school. Such a kit would contain the school's curriculum, a statement of the issues and current concerns of the school, the school's administrative procedures, and a faculty handbook. New faculty members preferred that orientation procedures be formally organized, planned, and clearly structured. There was a plea for the recognition and acceptance of their needs as learners, and for an allowance of time for orientation and self-development, time for them to plan specific educational experiences throughout the year as a means of reinforcement and integration, time for regular consultation with a senior faculty member, and time for further professional development as social work educators.

Some of the expressed concerns reflect the new faculty member's frustration because there was so little opportunity before reporting for work to learn in an orderly structured way the many things he had to know almost immediately. His frustration was suggestive of the feeling sometimes expressed by a new social work student as he moves into his first agency assignment. Reading between the lines, one can sense that the new teacher wanted help in finding his niche as a faculty member with his colleagues. He seemed to seek some sympathetic recognition that his awkwardness was not as total as it felt to him, and that his unsure beginning steps were leading him in the right direction.

Further, it seemed that once his struggles as a learner could be accepted as appropriate responses, that he was able to seek out tangible aids to help him in his new role, such as opportunities to observe an experienced teacher, or to participate in team teaching, help in curriculum building, course construction, in methods of teaching, in selection of learning experiences, and in ways of testing and evaluating outcomes. He felt freer to explore what was involved in faculty advising and in serving as liaison faculty to agency field instructors, and to request weekly conferences with a senior teacher, or regular group meetings of all the new faculty.

Another impression gleaned from the responses was the high motivation on the part of the new faculty member to become an effective teacher. It was clear that those who had answered the questionnaires were serious in their choice of a career in teaching and were eager to use a variety of resources to develop into competent teachers. Many new faculty members were frank in acknowledging their deficits in teaching skills and their lack of current substantive knowledge of curriculum content areas.

CONTRASTS IN ORIENTATION OF NEW FACULTY, NEW WORKERS TO AN AGENCY, AND STUDENTS TO THE PROFESSION

In social work practice, the process of orienting new workers in an agency is a familiar one and an activity in which social workers have developed special insights and skills. Agency executives are clear about the importance of having new workers know the history of the agency, the philosophy and goals of the agency. They want the new worker to know the policies and the ways in which the program of the agency can best be implemented; they want the new worker to feel comfortable, to have a desk of his own, to find his place quickly in the agency's social system, and to be helped to learn the special assignments given him. They particularly want to help him with questions or problems. Agencies have institutionalized the induction phase of a new worker's experience by calling it a probationary period, by assigning a lighter workload to enable a new worker to take on new responsibilities gradually as he becomes ready for them. A process of evaluation has become institutionalized so that as the new worker is helped to learn his new assignments, he is given feedback as to his progress. With a focus on the job as such, agencies have established clear policies about employment conditions, routes to promotion, and opportunities for self-development and professional advancement.

With regard to the new social work student, ways have been found to help him become oriented to the profession, to the school situation, and to the agency where he is placed for field instruction. Educators have found that some anxiety is functional and natural for the beginner, and that one way of dealing constructively with the anxiety is to give the beginner early assignments at a level that is manageable and within his capacity to perform. There is recognition that it is important for the beginner to know that he is expected to ask questions, to make mistakes, to need help. These aspects of dependency are not seen as signs of weakness, but rather as natural concomitants of being in an unfamiliar situation. The educator, in understanding the student's patterns of learning, has evolved some familiar guidelines, such as to begin where the student or learner is; build from the known to the unknown; proceed from the concrete to the abstract, and from the specific to the general, keeping the focus on the learner and his individual learning needs.

It would be simplistic to make a direct analogy between the new worker in an agency, the new student in the school of social work and the new faculty member. There are significant differences in terms of the life experiences and level of maturity, the knowledge, skills, and understanding which the individual brings to his assignment, and his demonstrated capacity for self-direction and self-development. But there are enough similarities involved in becoming a new faculty member that the insights and processes evolved in relation to new students and new workers can be usefully applied.

On several levels the special needs expressed by the new faculty member can be seen in relation to the knowledge gaps that he brings. One gap is a lack of information about the social work curriculum inasmuch as social work education has changed since he received his MSW. Another gap is the one that has developed as a result of his immersion in practice and his isolation from the academic community. Becoming a faculty member may mean literally "going back to school" for him, with all the discomforts that such a step may imply. Another knowledge gap is in the area of teaching; not only how to teach, but how to organize what one knows or needs to learn about his subject in order to select significant learning experiences and present them in a sequential orderly fashion.

The uncertainty of the new teacher, regardless of how competent he has been as a practitioner or an agency supervisor, places him in a vulnerable uncomfortable position. In many ways, current practices in the orientation of new teachers may seem by social work practice standards to be at an unsophisticated level. In social work practice, it is not acceptable to transmit social work skills through the apprenticeship route. In the preparation of new faculty there is a prevailing pattern of apprenticeship or in-service training. Too often there is an expectation that new faculty will learn on the job, catch-as-catch-can, by observation, by ad hoc conferences, by trial and error, by self-instruction, or by imitation of an experienced teacher.

AN ORIENTATION PROGRAM FOR NEW FACULTY

Eleven graduate schools responded in October, 1967, to a request from the Council to describe the orientation program of new faculty members. With material from these responses, and with the help of suggestions from

74

the new faculty members, it has been possible to construct some models for consideration and possible modification to meet the special needs of a given school. In their replies, the eleven schools expressed a conviction that carefully planned induction programs for new teachers were essential, and they were interested in knowing what other schools were doing and what guidelines could be developed in joint discussions.

Formal advanced education culminating in a doctoral degree provides an ideal comprehensive model. It requires three or more years. This preparation would precede the actual reporting for duty as a new teacher. Following such advancd pre-service preparation, the new faculty member would be equipped to begin as a new teacher and his orientation process would focus primarily on the institutional aspects of the specific university, school, and faculty as social systems that were new to him and within which he would find a place for himself.

The content of a typical orientation program can be divided into the following topics:

1. Knowledge of the school, its program, policies, its formal and informal structure.

2. Knowledge of the university, its program, services and facilities, and the relation of the school of social work to the total university.

3. Overview of the school curriculum, student body, field agencies, faculty assignments and responsibilities.

4. Knowledge of educational theories and methodology including knowledge of course construction, class management, examinations, and grading.

5. Acculturation to the social system of higher education, role expectations, routes for promotion.

6. Specific information as to assignments, whether in class or field, committee work, student advising, agency liaison.

7. Information as to employment conditions and benefits.

8. Information about the program and services of the Council on Social Work Education and the process of accreditation of schools.

The methods of involving a new faculty member in one or more of the above content areas of orientation can vary from an individual tutorial arrangement, whereby the new faculty member is assigned to a senior faculty member who takes responsibility for the planning and implementation of the orientation program in all its aspects, to a series of group experiences both within the school and on a larger geographical basis, whether regional or national.

The differentiation between group experiences within a given school and those held on a regional or national basis might result in having more general areas considered in regional and national sessions, and limiting the in-school matters to the local campus.

Whatever can be encompassed on a pre-service basis is to be recommended because the new teacher is confronted with new learning in so many areas. Such pre-service experiences can include a visit to the campus, a review of school minutes, selected curriculum and course materials, a copy of the faculty handbook, conferences with the dean and other faculty, attendance at faculty meetings, observation experiences in classes.

If it is at all possible to arrange for a semester or even a summer pre-service orientation, the new teacher can become acculturated to the school and university, to the curriculum, and to his own assignments. Time would be allowed for reading and updating of subject knowledge, for course preparation and for collateral reading in teaching and learning theories, and perhaps for some guided practice teaching.

Very useful would be a formal course or seminar for new teachers, for a semester or a summer, on a regional or national basis. A plan for independent study and self-development of the new teacher can be initiated and developed during this pre-service phase of orientation.

Once the new faculty member reports for duty, his orientation becomes a part of in-service preparation. Some complications which are involved in learning while doing may develop. It is incumbent on the school to plan carefully for the orientation program so that a new faculty member is encouraged to develop his own special interests within the framework of overall curriculum needs.

The in-service orientation will include general faculty developmental activities, but these cannot take the place of specially planned activities which focus on the orientation needs of new faculty members.

SUMMARY

In conclusion, there are growing indications that both the new faculty members and the administrative faculty in schools and departments will become more alert to the importance of having a carefully planned, well-organized program of pre-service as well as an in-service orientation that encompasses the objectives and implementation of the curriculum, the school and its larger campus, and the special demands of social work education. As new faculty members are helped to develop and to become more competent as teachers, benefits will accrue in the form of higher levels in the quality of teaching and in the professional growth of students, to the advantage of an improved social work practice in all areas.

ON BECOMING A TEACHER

by Virginia L. Tannar *

(A staff development or teaching position in a social agency does not involve the newness and complexity which is expected in moving to a new career in a university. The social agency is, in fact, familiar territory to the practitioner-turned-educator. Yet the changed role warrants analysis, so that its reality will not be neglected.

The following paper draws upon data from persons recently employed as teachers in social agencies as well as in schools of social work. It considers three aspects of the role transition. Ed.)

The major assumption of this paper is that teaching in the formal sense is an identifiable process with a knowledge base and involves skills which can be learned. The role of the teacher includes concern for the learner as well as concern for subject matter and method, conceptual mastery of the subject matter, and skills in communication, curriculum development, and organization.

Learning and teaching constitute a universal interactional process which goes on throughout the life span. The basic aspects of learning-teaching interaction relate to the life process and are developmental, maturational, experimental, and cognitive in nature. Differences in the age and stage of development of the learners affect the urgency of learning, the ease of learning, the continuities and discontinuities in learning and in teaching. The value a culture places on various ways of learning also affects the outcome of teaching.

The continuum begins in infancy and in early childhood with learning which is in the interest of survival of the individual as an organism. It continues through progressively more complex stages until it reaches the level at which there is the engaging of the conscious intelligence and attention of the individual. During the school and college years, a cultural as well as an academic expectation is that of learning how to learn. As the student learns to use findings from various sources and gains some insight

* Paper presented at the CSWE Sixteenth Annual Program Meeting on January 25, 1968, in Minneapolis, Minnesota. Miss Tannar is Staff Development Specialist, Children's Bureau, Social and Rehabilitation Service, U.S. Department of Health, Education, and Welfare.

into the learning process, he may in turn begin to develop his thinking about effective ways to teach.

The idea that good teachers are born and not made carries within it the element of individual expression, of creativity in teaching. The art in teaching is the way the teacher reveals his uniqueness and his creativity. Style then becomes the expression of the art of teaching. There is also the common observation that if one knows his subject, he can teach it. In today's highly specialized world, subject competence is a vital element. An additional factor in the mix which produces effective teachers is knowledge of the role of a teacher.

Some of the difficulty which beginning teachers face can be attributed to certain realities in the shift from practice or doctoral study to the role of teacher. In this paper, I have made use of comments and reactions from 22 persons who have recently been employed as teachers either in social agencies or in schools of social work. These individuals were asked to reply to questions in four major areas: a comparison between their last practice experience and their first teaching experience; the trouble spots in the transition from practice to teaching, either within the academic setting or the agency setting; the resources available to them in undertaking the role of a teacher; and recommendations for ways of assisting a person to become a teacher. The 22 persons gave thoughtful and stimulating answers to these questions. It is important to say that their reactions cannot be taken as representative of the entire group of recently appointed faculty or persons appointed to staff development positions in public welfare agencies. The letters do, however, give useful data about what it is like to assume the role of a teacher.

Three aspects of the role transition are considered: (1) the import of authority, academic freedom, and control in the teaching situation and the administrative structure within which these factors are played out; (2) knowledge and skills and the different uses made of them in teaching; and (3) self-image and feelings about the role.

Authority and Academic Freedom

The problem of authority, academic freedom, and control is an important first consideration in role transition from practice to teaching. At the time when the decision is made to shift from practice to teaching, the professional social worker already has some well-patterned ways of responding to authority and control in his freedom of thought and action. In assuming the role of teacher, either in the academic or agency setting, one finds that there are certain differences in the use of knowledge and of self. Knowledge has different authority in a teaching situation. Academic freedom is frequently experienced by the beginning teacher as a different kind of self-responsibility, of professional discipline. Habits of thought, feeling, and ac-

78

tion associated with the bureaucratic behavior learned within an agency may persist for two or three years. The shift from these patterns to the new experience as a teacher in either setting demands of the individual considerable self-assessment of the extent and depth of his knowledge and of his potential capacity to undertake the double demand for professional identification as social worker and as educator. The degree of freedom is usually welcomed by the new teacher, but some of the implications of academic freedom—of being on one's own in new ways, of the more complex and subtle changes in the authority-dependency syndrome—are a source of initial stress in the role transition.

As one new faculty member expressed it, "I found it very disconcerting at first to sit in faculty meetings and hear a variety of ideas and points of view expressed by faculty members without any coming together or consensus in regard to these ideas and without any position being taken in regard to the overall planning and direction which the school might take in these matters. . . . It still seems like a ponderous and very slow moving process to me and is certainly dramatically different from the agency setting where administration makes all the decisions."

In the academic setting, the degree to which educational policy is determined by the faculty as a whole is an indicator of academic freedom. Although there is a national guideline for curriculum development, the issue still remains for individual faculty members. There are distinct charges, rights, responsibilities, and privileges assigned to faculty according to the administrative structure of the university and the school of social work and the legal and professional standards by which academic freedom is judged in each university or college.

In addition, since schools of social work are concerned with graduate professional education, other guides have to be internalized. These guides include the goals of the particular school and the values and ethics of the profession of social work. Included also are the values of the university setting which include scholarship and the pursuit of excellence. Similarly, freedom and control within the teacher's role in an agency influences the nature of the transition from practitioner to agency teacher. The federal policy established in 1962 states that persons undertaking the teaching of social workers in public welfare agencies are required to have an MSW from an accredited school of social work. Practice experience is also required. Thus the teachers must meet educational requirements as well as achieve professional identification. Herein lies a possible source of conflict for the agency teacher in public welfare settings. As one teacher explained: "The issue becomes that of how much an agency makes use of social work knowledge and skill." A basic question deals with how fully the authority inherent in professional knowledge and professional competence will be permitted by the agency to guide the activities of the agency teacher.

Of course, the agency teacher's authority and functions are based essentially on the goals and program of the agency. The purpose of staff development is to provide training oriented to specific jobs. The teacher's job is often considered to be a "staff position" rather than a "line position," that is, it is not lodged within a long chain of command. The agency teacher is allowed a wide latitude, or almost complete authority, in the selection of content and methods and allotment of time for achieving objectives. For some agency teachers, the granting of this freedom means a period of self-searching, of delving into one's professional commitment and knowledge, of re-examination of what professional authority entails in order to build another kind of self-confidence. This might be described as a freer use of professional standards, of oneself as a professional person away from activities controlled largely by detailed rules, instructions, and procedures. As one person stated, "There is increased responsibility for accountability to professional values and ethics in being an agency teacher as compared to being an agency supervisor."

Another clearly identified difference between the two positions is that the satisfactions which came with "decision-making authority" in administrative supervision on a case-by-case basis are no longer part of the agency teacher's life. As one person expressed it, "The loss of administrative and supervisory authority was one of the most difficult adjustments, particularly since my office remained in the county where I formerly supervised. To observe my successor struggling with or ignoring a task which I would have liked to do has required considerable discipline. I have also missed keenly the authority I formerly had in being able to follow through with individual staff members to insure better performance."

In the teacher role, the source of job satisfaction is no longer immediate feedback from visible results of personal influence, direction, and guidance. The results of effective teaching may not be observable for weeks, nor can they be easily measured. The agency teacher is further removed from the outcome for the individual client and must direct a good part of his concern for the client and the program toward a third party, a trainee.

The role of the agency teacher is further influenced by the fact that he may be one of only a few persons with this function in the agency. In some instances he may be the only person who is an agency teacher. The proportion of staff to agency teachers varies but is likely to be at least 200 to one. The ratio is kept high by the scarcity of qualified teaching personnel and the lack of funded positions. As the only person, or one of very few persons, with the teaching function, the agency teacher has limited opportunity to learn from others who carry teaching responsibility. This tends to add to the loneliness of the role. Furthermore, certain administrative attitudes and practices may contribute to the isolation of the agency teacher.

Balanced against these role changes which may be experienced as loss, as stress, or as isolation, are other aspects of the teacher's role. The role gives one a potential for influence in overall policy "even without direct authority over any one." The role means wider channels of communication, both with administration and with other staff. It includes the authority of a specialist and it allows for extensive use of professional knowledge and indirect influence as well as direct influence in program, in policy, and in working for uniformity and consistency in practice.

In contrast to the agency teacher, the new faculty member is admitted to a company of peers. Potentially he has access to experienced teachers for guidance, in a variety of areas: course content, objectives, methods of presentation, student learning problems, curriculum problems, and overcoming the "butterflies" which he may have when he undertakes his first class. Senior faculty may be officially designated as mentors to new faculty. In this way support and encouragement is available to the new faculty member.

Knowledge and Skill in Teaching

The new teacher in either the academic or agency setting usually does take a new reading on what he has as his foundation in knowledge and skill. This re-examination uncovers gaps, unevenness, even blanks, and motivates the new teacher to "expand" his knowledge. As one person in the aforementioned survey stated, "I was forced to widen my horizons, and intellectually expand and grow in a variety of directions and areas, but I found this to be very stimulating." This necessity to increase one's depth and range of knowledge pushes the beginning teacher into "catching up" with the literature, seeking better understanding of newer theoretical constructs, exploring innovative practice. It is a process that should be continuous and one that characterizes the high degree of intellectual curiosity which is the mark of a good teacher.

Certain problems about the knowledge base, however, characterize the initial phases in becoming a teacher. Vast amounts of knowledge are available to any beginning teacher but there is no scheme either in schools of social work or within agencies which allows for a quick systematic retrieval of this knowledge. The problem is not only one of obtaining access to the knowledge but also that of assessing the reliability of the information and the soundness of the philosophy underlying the principles set forth. In schools of social work, guidance is available through the faculty system of building the curriculum and through committee structure, current course outlines, bibliographies, past assignments, sequence committees, and consultation. An agency teacher, however, is in a less favorable position because the system of staff development is just beginning to be structured, and, therefore, there is less guidance available for such technical assistance.

There is also the problem for beginning teachers of translating knowledge

—scientific, theoretical, or practical—into language which is understandable to the learner. He must help groups of learners to use this material to build on what they already know. Here the first demand is that the learner be helped to make the connection between conceptual thinking and practice.

A new demand on the practitioner-turned-teacher is setting goals in teaching, the business of curriculum and course planning. New skills to be learned include preparing the lecture, learning how to deliver it, making course outlines, compiling bibliographies, and preparing assignments. In learning these skills, a consistent theoretical framework for curriculum development which covers objectives, content, learning experiences, and evaluative measures is needed.

The teaching of groups in a formal setting for the first time may also make demands on the new teacher. Often teachers enter the classroom "with little appreciation for the dynamic aspects of group learning." As the teacher experiences the interaction among group members and between the group and himself, and as he begins to feel the force of group cohesion and group response, he becomes acutely conscious of the need for a framework for understanding and using the cues from the group. One agency teacher put this problem in these terms: "What I was not fully prepared for was the impact of moving from the comfort and freedom of the one-to-one experience to the classroom. How to convey the teacher image, the authority, and competency implied by this role was one of my concerns."

A grasp of learning theory and instructional theory is essential so that teaching behavior can be consciously controlled and directed toward specific ends. However, learning to think in a more structured way about how to use knowledge for the purposes of instruction is a new skill to the beginning teacher and requires practice, feedback from the learners, and willingness on the part of the instructor to receive the reactions of his learners with an open mind.

Self-Image and Feelings About New Role

The new teacher also has a changed professional status to which he must adjust. The move to formal teaching is often considered a move upward, and there may, in fact, be a promotion involved, a more prestigious title, or a higher salary. The individual may have been chosen from a group of peers to become a teacher and this also adds prestige. In the academic setting, however, the move from practice to teaching is likely to have some elements that stress one's beginning position; the title may impress on the new teacher that this is a shift from a position with an earned high rank to a position of low rank in the academic hierarchy. In the agency ranking system, depending upon the individual agency structure, a teaching position may carry higher status even at a beginning level. When one is detached from his previous role and is not yet fully admitted to the new role, the need for the support of status and rank is likely to be increased.

What then may beginning teachers expect in the way of feelings about their new role? For some, there is a sense of being overwhelmed by the theoretical base of what is being taught. Just becoming familiar with the new sets of theories in social work and related fields seems a large order. But there is also the immediate pressure of being ready for next Monday's class. Along with this some feel that the job of teacher does "give one the opportunity to try out one's ideas and be creative."

Another challenge is the feeling of obligation to the learners. One new teacher reported that teachers have "some uneasiness that students are being shortchanged by reason of the teacher's lacks in knowledge and in skill in teaching" but that "the more ideas they tried out which were successful, the more confidence and competence increased." Personal satisfaction comes from conducting a successful class, from being exposed to the learners' enthusiasm and commitment to serve people. Many young people coming into schools of social work and agencies today have a strong desire to serve, to involve themselves in a dynamic way in helping clients. Unfortunately there is a scarcity of persons qualified to teach these students and trainees.

We have considered the numerous needs and problems that people face as they enter the world of teaching. Ultimately it is up to the agencies and schools to make it possible to enable teachers to fulfill their potential. We have a responsibility to call attention to the needs of beginning teachers and propose ways of meeting them. I feel confident that this is a responsibility we will increasingly recognize and carry out.

PRACTICES AND PROBLEMS IN THE SELECTION AND DEVELOPMENT OF FACULTY FOR SCHOOLS OF SOCIAL WORK

("Practices and Problems in the Selection and Development of Faculty for Schools of Social Work," was the theme for a session at the CSWE Thirteenth Annual Program Meeting. The scope of the five papers presented included both pre-service preparation and induction concerns and practices. The three excerpted papers utilized here fall more directly within our immediate focus on the induction period. The three authors, though faculty members from the same school, were each speaking from a different vantage point, one as a vice-dean, the second as a new faculty member coming from an agency setting, and the third as a veteran teacher new to the school. Other presentations made at this session were by Marie McNaobla of the Social Work Section, Training Division, National Institute of Mental Health, whose programs include support for doctoral study and "career teacher" fellowships as preparation for educational careers, and Dr. Simone Pare, director of a school of social work in Canada. Ed.)

INTRODUCTION OF SPEAKERS

by Ruth E. Smalley *

The selection and development of faculty is a problem not only for our own and other professional schools, but for universities and colleges generally. . . . That it is a problem is being increasingly recognized and identified.[1]

. . . It is interesting to speculate whether professional schools—specifically, schools of social work—have a more or less difficult task than academic departments in the preparation and induction of faculty. Social work faculties are drawn largely from professional practice rather than from recently completed programs of academic study. This is a potential strength and richness,

---

[1] For details, see section on "Responses to the Problems of Quantity and Quality in Preparation for University Careers," in *Faculty Development in Professional Education*, by Joseph Soffen (New York: Council on Social Work Education, 1967), pp. 37-44.

---

* Excerpts from three papers presented at the CSWE Thirteenth Annual Program Meeting on January 30, 1964, in Toronto, Ontario, Canada. Dr. Smalley was then dean of the School of Social Work, University of Pennsylvania.

as well as a potential problem. Yet even though most new social work faculty come directly from practice, some are inducted following doctoral study in a school of social work with or without a specific concentration in teaching as a focus of their doctoral program.

What is involved, what is facilitating, what is necessary from the point of view of the seeking and inducting school to help a professional practitioner, a recent graduate of a social work doctoral program with or without a concentration in teaching, or a member of another discipline or profession become an effective teacher in a school of social work? It is to these questions and others which they may evoke that Dr. Wessel's paper is addressed.

But it is not alone a question of the selecting and inducting school's responsibility to find new faculty and then to create the conditions and to provide the personnel, the structure, and the process through which a teacher may develop. There is also the responsibility of the one who is selected to become, in fact, a teacher, a teacher in a particular area or areas, and in a particular school. Eric Fromm writes of the "decisive act which we alone can perform, the 'courage to be,' the jump, the act of ultimate commitment, an act without which no real change occurs in a human being."

What is involved for the new teacher, both the teacher new to teaching and the teacher who comes to a school different from the one he left and to a teaching area new to him if he is to make that kind of jump—the responsible act of commitment, in addition to mastering necessary knowledge and teaching skill? What is involved if he is to achieve human and committed competence, as well as technical competence as a teacher in a school of social work? Dr. Berg and Dr. Soffen draw upon their own experiences and suggest hypotheses to be examined and tested by others.

AS VIEWED BY ONE SCHOOL

by Rosa Wessel*

(In this excerpt, Dr. Wessel describes the specialization for teachers within the doctoral program of the University of Pennsylvania School of Social Work, as well as general practices for the induction of teachers into the school. In this context, doctoral study is conceived as a consciously designed program for inducting the candidate into a teaching career. In addition, there is an emphasis upon helping all new faculty move into the school through a mentorship arrangement. Ed.)

The planning for buildings, now going up at an astonishing pace on many campuses, has absorbed a great deal of faculty interest and time, especially on administrative levels; but now the day of reckoning is upon us. We have forecast possible and desirable increases in enrollment over the next ten years, but what begins to face us as a reality now is the necessity to plan for corresponding increase in faculty. Faculty recruitment is usually carried out, as one dean has said, as a "fire-fighting project," but we are determined to be more planful and to make it a long-term program of selection and development; and we have already made a beginning.

We know of course that there is no pool of teachers, fully prepared with specialized knowledge, with successful experience in a variety of social work and social welfare programs, with scholarly as well as creative interests and aptitudes, with versatility and flexibility, and with teaching skill, into which we can dip. We have further accepted that each school has to contribute to the continuing development of its own faculty—of each individual member, whatever his competence, as well as of the whole ensemble.

Thoughtful selection presupposes some prior decisions about the nature and purpose of the program of education that a school hopes to provide. The 1962 Curriculum Policy Statement, the end product of much professional collaboration in which we have all played a part, and to which we are therefore self-committed, is fortunately a basic guide to content. We do know that for social work we need educators who comprehend deeply some matters which do not yield their truth to the operations of the abacus. I refer especially to the human spirit in its striving for a more ideal world; for at bottom such is the motivation of almost every student in our schools

---

* Dr. Wessel was vice-dean of the School of Social Work, University of Pennsylvania, when this paper was delivered. She retired in 1966.

of social work; the motivation is comprised of great visions and dreams, which can be made to wither at their source when not valued and fostered by teachers who are also visionaries and dreamers as well as practical men.

To paraphrase Thoreau, we need men "who see present things as if past and future, as if distant or universally significant." These words identify the teacher with the poet in his outlook upon life; but they are not intended as a denial of the scholar. By common agreement scholarliness is an attribute highly desirable in a faculty member. It is the coin of free communication within a faculty body, even between faculty members of diverse disciplines. Itself a value, it provides a common approach to the seeking of knowledge, and a common base for the valuing of knowledge—of what is significant and what is relevant, or even of what may be true or false.

. . . Here I believe is the pivot of our problem. Do we really identify ourselves as teachers—educators—or as social workers? My own experience is probably not too unusual. I had taught at the "Pennsylvania School" for many years without any study or knowledge of educational theory, identifying myself always as a social worker. Upon undertaking doctoral study I decided I ought to know something about the process which I had carried intuitively for so many years. By great good fortune I was exposed through a brilliant historian and philosopher to the history of education down the ages, beginning with primitive man, through Sumeria, through Greece and Rome, through the early Christian era, the Dark Ages and the Middle Ages, the Reformation and Renaissance, the Age of Enlightenment, and on to the present. Thus I found my identification with the changing purposes, problems, and processes of the educator; and I made a new alignment with the university, this time as teacher.

What I learned also to identify more explicitly, and therefore to value anew, were the educational philosophy and principles by which I had been informally and unknowingly inducted into teaching, through my close association with the team of Robinson-Taft-Pray and deSchweinitz, which had created the school where I had been first student and then teacher. In its simplest terms the philosophy of education-through-doing, involving the whole person of the student, his powers of both intellect and feeling, whatever its earlier roots, can still be called the John Dewey philosophy. It is as basic to the school today as it was when I first entered it. This fact determines in large measure the quality of person who has been sought and whom we now continue to seek for the faculty. For it requires of a teacher a human interest in the student, in the student's use of the educational experience, and the power to evoke his response, both intellectual and emotional, to the educational content taught.

Let no one be under the illusion that it is easy to make a major shift of setting, from the world of practice to the academic world, and the change in the use of self that is required. It is the practice at our school to appoint a senior member of the faculty as mentor for each newly appointed faculty member. Since I am the oldest member of the faculty in point of service, my experience in that position has been extensive. For all their desire and choice to teach, for all the voluntary preparation that has necessarily gone into leaving a successful job, always one of importance, usually high in the administrative hierarchy, whether they come to us directly from the job or from doctoral study, they experience the actual shift somewhat drastically. They find it difficult to get a "toe-hold," and they experience a sense of being on the outside—a sense of "you" and "me" and a long distance intervening. Nothing symbolizes this new teacher's loss of self-orientation so much as the almost empty mailbox in the faculty distributor in the early months, or the necessity to share a secretary with a group of instructors—he who has often been accustomed to "calling the tune" with a secretary of his own who could be summoned by the pressing of a button. I have been over this same painful ground with more than one new faculty member, while he struggled to discover where he could make the break-through that would let him feel truly in, acting out of his own creative, active, achieving self.

In our weekly planned conferences—oftener if necessary—we have discussed the content of his teaching, his organization of it, and his proposed method for presenting it. And when he has met his classes we have discussed not only the development of the content but also his attitude toward and his relations with the students individually and as a group. We have also worked together on how he could devise some method for recording each student's developmental experience. He has been required to keep some kind of running record of the development of his own course from week to week. If he is a teacher of a practice course he is helped to make his connection with field agencies and field supervisors. We share with him the school's relationship with each, helping him to learn the resources of the school's files from which he can learn much useful data about them. He is helped to make the necessary connections with the other instructors of his students, with whom his teaching constantly dovetails in an integrative pattern. We try also to help him find his voice in faculty meetings, encouraging him to own, value, and express his difference.

As part of the process of introduction, whether to teaching or, if he has taught previously, to teaching at this school, we have held the new teacher's assignment to a minimal load—during the first year—usually one or two classes. Thus we give him time to familiarize himself with the professional literature which is liberally used in teaching, and with the use of our well-stocked library as a tool in teaching. He has time to read his students' papers slowly, even ponderously, as at first it seems necessary in order to catch both content and meaning, and to experiment with and discuss the kind of comment he wishes to make in response, whether positive or negative, to facilitate the students' learning.

Need I add that this kind of planned, steady help, welcome and much needed as it is, stirs also the other side—reactivates resistance to what has reminiscent overtones of what has felt like a long outgrown form of supervision, and its accompanying fear of being fettered by the authoritative control of another person? These feelings seem all the more acute at moments when the new teacher feels his own ineptness and his need for help —when he feels he has taught a session poorly, has handled a student badly, has missed an opportunity to lift a discussion to a higher level of abstraction—hasn't perhaps even seen the opportunity, himself. And the hurt of his betrayal of his human vulnerability before another person is not easy for him to bear. He may well long for the familiar comfort of operating with a known process, directly with his own clients or staff. There are times when he will confess to feeling trapped in "the ivory tower," with its oppressive silences, when it seems that everyone else is in a classroom or working behind a closed door.

I have been giving you the content and the mood of weekly conferences, especially in the critical early weeks and months. Though I have emphasized the experiences of the teacher who is new to the process of teaching, much that I have said applies also to any teacher who moves into a new school even after substantial experience. For beginnings are, after all, beginnings —and who should know the precariousness of this period better than social workers? Since it is the students who pay the price of the teacher's inexperience and insecurity, we have used our knowledge about process in helping the teacher for the students' sake, as well as for his own.

There is a strong feeling among the schools of social work against standardization of doctoral programs, and in support of each school developing its own program in relation to its own particular strengths. The doctoral programs, therefore, show great diversity, some emphasizing research, some the social sciences, some advanced clinical competence, some community organization. Yet we do know about the doctoral graduates of all of these schools, that whatever their specialization in doctoral study may have been, sooner or later most of them have moved into teaching. Indeed, many of them, as the emphasis upon doctoral qualifications has grown, have come into doctoral study from the schools, with the intention of becoming better qualified to remain in teaching.

From the beginning of our own doctoral program in 1949, the University of Pennsylvania School has recognized the choice of specialization in teaching of some doctoral students. Since the first year of the doctoral program includes advanced field study in an area of practice, we have provided as many candidates as possible with a supervised teaching opportunity within our own school. Each has full responsibility, under supervision, for one class in one area of the curriculum throughout the year, and attends all general faculty meetings as well as special group faculty meetings. Necessarily these

89

opportunities are limited. In a few instances we have given the same kind and quality of supervision to some of our advanced students who are faculty members of other schools of social work, and whose teaching of one course in their own schools is used for advanced field study.

All doctoral students take a year-long course in Social Work Processes, which includes discussion and reading about the process of teaching in social work. When there are students who have teaching assignments in the class, the discussion of their own recorded experience with their assigned class becomes a part of the content of the advanced Processes course. The continuous supervision by a senior faculty member extends throughout this year, and the student ends this experience by writing a substantial project reflecting his study in depth in the area of teaching. They are also advised to study the history or philosophy of education or related courses in the University's Graduate School of Education. From this kind of pursuit of the relation of the program of social work education to all educational forms have come a number of valuable doctoral dissertations.

Have I answered some of Dr. Smalley's questions? We are sure of the quality of the faculty members we are seeking—we want only superior people, and we include both intellectual and emotional qualities in our evaluation. We want, for the most part, people who come from the practice of social work; but if not, we want people who are deeply related to our professional values and purposes. We want men who see life as a complete culture, in both its scientific and humanistic aspects, who see life as both a vision and an activity. We want people who are interested in teaching, in communicating what they know, in the way that stimulates students to question, to study, to grow. We want people who, if they do not already have this competence, are willing to learn. We know some of the hazards along the way for the person who moves from one position to another, whether from practice or the academic life, into our own school; but we are sure that we know how to help overcome many of these hazards.

AS VIEWED BY
A NEW FACULTY MEMBER NEW TO FULL-TIME TEACHING

by Renee Berg*

These are my own experiences in becoming a teacher; unique, therefore, but, as is true of any personal experience, with aspects that may be meaningful to other people in similar situations. Dean Smalley said, in her introductory statement, that social work faculty are drawn largely from the profession. The long journey from social agency practitioner to school of social work faculty member, which I have recently undertaken, will be made by increasing numbers in the future, in response to the need for expanded educational facilities in our field. Before talking about what this change was like for me, I shall describe briefly the background from which I came into full-time teaching in the fall of 1962—three 15-week terms ago, as I have now learned to reckon time.

I had worked in agencies more than 20 years, a few as caseworker, many more as supervisor of students, workers, and other supervisors. In my last four years of agency employment I supervised units of students of a school of social work but as a staff member of the agency in which the students were doing their field work. I had fairly extensive teaching experience in addition to that inherent in supervision: in agency in-service training programs, in institutes, and in classes for employed workers in the school with which I am now associated. I did not have a concentration in teaching during my doctoral work, but as part of my first term of teaching a non-credit course, I had the advantage of weekly conferences with an experienced and gifted teacher to help me learn to teach.

Coming with this much teaching experience and with so many years of association with the school of social work itself, as an agency colleague and a part-time faculty member, I did not anticipate much dislocation in moving into full-time teaching. I was wrong. I found there was a great difference between coming and going at the school, while based in an agency, and staying and belonging, as I am still learning to do. When I earlier used the term "long journey" to describe the distance between practice and teaching, I did so advisedly.

What are the elements of this dislocation? First, there is the inevitable accompaniment of all beginnings: that one must leave the old. I worked with surety and competence in agency settings; I knew my way around.

* Dr. Berg is on the faculty of the School of Social Work, University of Pennsylvania.

Supervising students in field work, where learning takes place in the reality of giving an agency's service, was always deeply interesting to me. It was a jolt to leave all this for the tentativeness and unfamiliarity of a new role. I found it strange to answer "teacher" instead of "social worker" in reply to questions about my occupation, and the first few times I felt somewhat an imposter, and a rather reluctant one at that. To a degree, I have had to build a new identity.

Making the transition from agency to educational institution involves taking on a new set of imperatives. In an agency, every activity finds purpose, meaning, direction, from the agency's reason for existence: service to clients. Every activity in a school must, of course, relate itself to the school's central purpose: education of students for the profession. This means different content, different emphases, different pressures, a different rhythm to one's work life—a whole new orientation. Although I am increasingly aware of myself as an educator, with an educator's concerns, and although I have never worked harder than since becoming a faculty member, I discover in myself the lingering remnants of old prejudices. I find myself sometimes thinking scornfully of the solidity of agency versus ivory towers, and of those who can, and do, versus those who can't, and teach. Then I remind myself where I have cast my lot, that it is no longer *them* of whom I am saying this, but *us*, and make a fresh start.

Thus far I have been talking only about the aspects of becoming a teacher in a school of social work which I have found unfamiliar and difficult. Of course, this is not the whole picture. The part that feels comfortable and relatively known is of such importance that it makes it possible to bear more or less patiently with the problems. I refer to the direct contact with the students, through the activities of classroom teaching and serving as faculty adviser. More than once during the past year I have said lightly that I enjoy teaching but I'm not sure I like being an educator. I realize now that in making this distinction—a purely personal one, unblessed by Webster— I have assigned to the category of teacher all those activities that involve me with the students; to that of educator, the multifarious ones essential to supporting this central activity.

I think it is likely that most persons coming from the field to a school would be best prepared for the area of actual teaching. Many of them would have been interested as agency staff members in assignments with teaching components, such as supervision and staff training. Although the responsibilities of a teacher in a school of social work are different and course content differs and must be learned, there is much in the method and skill of teaching which remains unchanged. The give and take of the classroom, the use of oneself in presenting material in such a way that the student is enabled to learn, the inter-relationship between teacher and class, all call on skills that are part of the professional equipment of the agency practitioner.

It follows too that the counseling the faculty adviser does with individual students is familiar ground, different only in that it is focused on the student's educational progress. Also, it is in the actual teaching that agency and client come back into view, with one's constant awareness that whatever the content of the course being taught, it carries the weight of *professional* and is being taught not as knowledge for its own sake, but for the student to use in becoming a professional social worker. Not surprisingly, it was in teaching casework practice class that I first felt at home.

I want here to underline my point that the transition from social work practitioner to social work educator is neither quick nor easy. Others following the same route may well encounter their difficulties in different areas, but I suspect that the difficulties will be there and, perhaps, the more firmly rooted in professional practice the candidate for teacher is, the more difficult the transition. What can the school of social work offer as aids to induction, to the leading in of the new faculty member, so that he or she can truly become one, instead of simply having been named one by the appointing authority? Again, I am speaking out of my own experience.

Having a modified work load in the first year was very helpful. When one is doing everything for the first time, when nothing comes naturally, as it were, one moves at a pace much slower than one is accustomed to. To have to carry a full quota of teaching and committee assignments would have, I believe, been an impossible task. I was not aware of this as I began my first year, not being prepared, as I have already said, for the degree to which full-time teaching would be strange and different. In fact, my unexpressed reaction, when the dean told me of this modified assignment, was that this was very kind, but I really did not need to be protected. It was only later that I realized how very much I did need to be!

The opportunity which I had, and took full advantage of, for weekly conferences with the director of first year was invaluable. There was great comfort and helpfulness in having an established time, place, and person for my seemingly endless questions. Perhaps even more important than the answers to the questions was the other use I could make of this time: testing my thinking with someone I respected and trusted. Without this latter, the uncertainties of the "first time round" would have been quite overwhelming.

I am amused now when I recall how surprised I was to discover that there were organized ways of doing things—structures—at the school, even as there were in agencies. Perhaps, as is often true of beginners, I felt that everything would have to start afresh with me. I was relieved, however, that this was not so. I mention this because I know from my own experience that people familiar with a job carry a lot of it in their heads and can forget how important it is for the new person that as much as possible be regularized and written down.

Of a different nature, but very important to my induction, was receiving a welcome which not only recognized and provided for my newness and slowness, but also valued and used the special knowledge I brought precisely because I was new to education and fresh from the field.

I could summarize what I have said up to this point very quickly: some aspects of my move from agency to school have been easier, others have been harder. This presents us with a kind of balance sheet, and leaves untouched the important question: Do I want to be a full-time teacher? Is there anything about teaching that weighs the balance in its favor? In short, why teaching? Loren Eiseley writes beautifully and appropriately of the educator who,

> . . . amid contingencies and weariness, without mental antennae, and with tests that fail him, is a savior of souls. He is giving shapes to time, and the shapes themselves, driven by their own inner violence, wrench free of his control—must, if they are truly sculptured, surge like released genii from the classroom or, tragically, shrink to something less than bottle size.[1]

"He is giving shapes to time, and the shapes themselves, driven by their own inner violence, wrench free of his control. . . ." Teaching is a creative act and, for some of us—who knows why—the most satisfying form of creation. Eiseley's words describe the essence of this creative activity and of the teacher's relationship to those he teaches. The shapes will indeed wrench free, and it is part of the joy of teaching that they will do this. Indeed, one strives to liberate that "inner violence." But, nevertheless, in some small way one shapes the future, one's vision of what is humanly (and therefore professionally) good and desirable is conveyed to others and, transformed, carried into the unknown future.

---

[1] Loren Eiseley, *The Mind as Nature* (New York and Evanston: Harper & Row, 1962), pp. 24-25.

AS VIEWED BY
A FACULTY MEMBER WITH EXPERIENCE IN ANOTHER SCHOOL

by Joseph Soffen

The invitation to prepare this paper is for me a special opportunity, for in recollecting the experience of moving from one school to the University of Pennsylvania I have been making an assessment which, at the very least, is most valuable for me. Hopefully, some of my observations may be useful to others.

I have recast the question posed to me into a proposition which has two parts. The first part states that the school and any inductee have certain concerns, whether the inductee is new to teaching or is changing schools. Obviously the school wants any inductee to find his place within the faculty, so that he can strengthen it and be strengthened by it. All will have concerns about salary, personnel practices, and the conditions which are conducive to professional satisfactions and growth.

The second part of the proposition states that both the school and the recruit with previous teaching experience at another school have a special stake over and above that involved in the induction of a faculty member new to the academic setting. The school presumably wants, and reasonably can expect, to benefit from previous experience which the inductee brings and which it recognizes symbolically by the higher rank which is offered him. The latter, in turn, reasonably expects a climate which permits him to make his unique contribution—a sense that he can have a constructive impact on the institution to which he has come—that his coming has made a difference. He wants the difference which his past represents to be valued by the new institution, while at the same time wanting to become a citizen of the new institution, albeit a naturalized one, with the rights and obligations of full citizenship.

I am therefore suggesting that all inductees, whether or not with previous teaching experience, share concerns that arise from coming to a new institution and new responsibilities. The school, in turn, has the same concerns for both kinds of recruits. But in addition, it is necessary to acknowledge that the person with previous teaching experience feels that there are special expectations of him and he must deal with these expectations.

What are the implications of these expectations? Will the orientation differ from that normally available to one newly recruited to the academic setting? Is the "know-how" from one university setting an asset or an impediment in a different university? To what extent can transfer of skill be expected where the major identification has been—in my case, as an example—with a group work program with responsibilities for the development of field work resources, teaching graduate, extension, and undergraduate courses primarily in group work, to a primary assignment in teaching research at the master's and advising at the doctoral level? Are there problems inherent in a move from a program with which I was associated almost from its inception to an established department in one of the earliest established schools? In this instance, the move was to a school with a distinctive history and tradition.

Let me attempt to answer some of these questions by describing some of the ingredients which it seemed to me the school consciously provided to minimize the risks and to free me to make of the transition an opportunity to achieve what both I and the school were seeking. Ours has been a happy experience, so that it is neither difficult nor inappropriate to share some of the intimate details—at any rate those from which some generalizations can be drawn which others may find helpful.

The induction process, in fact, unfolded over a period of two years—not in one week or even one semester—and consisted of a sequence of phases, differing from each other in depth and in quality. The quality of these phases may be characterized as: (1) talking, (2) doing, and (3) feeling. The preliminary phase of induction actually began during my first discussion with Dean Smalley, considerably prior to any negotiations or sense of contract. I was invited to spend a carefully scheduled day at the school. I talked with the dean for only a few minutes at the beginning and end of the day. Most of the talking was with the people with whom I would be working—the chairman and members of the research department. In addition, time was scheduled for individual conferences with senior professors in the several sequences. Perhaps the word "talking" should be broadened to include reading —course descriptions, completed student research projects, and theses. There was lunch with a group of faculty members, most of whom I was not seeing by individual appointment. Before the end of the day I had met a large percentage of the faculty—all of whom could be available that day. Of course, they were all "looking me over," and I was looking them over. But more important, it seems to me, the structure provided for meeting individually. The interchanges in each of the several conferences supplemented each other, and the richness of the day's meetings attests to the fact that we were able to go beyond superficial greetings and polite generalities. As a result, subsequent negotiations were not with the dean of an abstract institution but of a faculty whose claim to my respect was based on the most important evidence for me—not their reputations but direct contact with them.

The second phase, characterized by "doing," began three months before the beginning of the school year. I was invited to spend a day in June at the school, although classes do not begin until September. At this time we discussed the specifics of my assignment for the coming year. My office had

96

already been designated and my name was already in place over the door. The psychological impact of this early visit is not to be minimized. The visual evidence that my coming was being planned for stimulated for me a sense of the reality of the new assignment and provided a focus for planning during the summer months. Being put on the payroll starting July 1 was a helpful detail which should also be acknowledged. Psychologically, as well as officially, I was now on duty.

Instead of starting with a full complement of teaching and committee responsibilities, which would later constitute my typical assignment, I was given only a three-quarter load. We all know the theory that favors giving a new worker a reduced load initially so that he may be free to learn his way about a new setting or a new job. I have taught this theory in courses on administration. But in some half-dozen professional settings in which I have been a beginner, this was the only time I had experienced this bit of theory translated into administrative practice. On the contrary, I had seen some of the most tedious and least inspiring tasks of agency life earmarked for the person with least seniority. I am not unaware of the conviction that is required to justify a reduced load at the highest administrative levels within the university. How was the time and energy freed by the reduced load utilized?

My load was sufficiently reduced so that I could participate as a learner in a pivotal course, at the doctoral level, not as an observer or auditor but as an active participant. This course did not have to compete with other responsibilities. Tuesday afternoon from 2:00 to 3:40 was earmarked on my schedule, with the same official aura as was Wednesday morning, when I met one of my classes as teacher. I was responsible for preparing all assignments—readings, papers, and presentations to the class. My role in the class was explained to the other class members.

We had considered possible counterindications to this arrangement before attempting it. What might be the negatives from the point of view of the instructor of the course, the other members of the class, or mine? We looked for them and noted at times that there was obviously something different in the class because of my participation in it. But this difference was not substantive, and no one was called upon to pay any discernible price as a result. True, I had to produce and the instructor had to produce. But we were both willing to risk this, and for me, at any rate, it was very productive.

What had I gained? Let us grant that every school has distinctive qualities, in its philosophy and methods of teaching, over and beyond what it holds in common with sister institutions. Appropriate orientation helps the recruit to identify that part of the new setting which is familiar as well as that which is different and which he will need to learn (he finds, incidentally, that more is familiar than he might have anticipated). I had an opportunity to experience, in a most intimate way, what it was like being a student at this school—no mean asset to any teacher! The orientation extended over a whole year, rather than in a "crash" program. The focus for reading provided by the course was useful. In addition, I suspect that this type of participation in a class is at least as meaningful, if not more so, for the person who has had teaching experience, as for the person newly entering into teaching. He can use his own skill as a teacher for testing the learning experiences of the course. An unusual opportunity for in-service training!

I now come to an item of administration which is pertinent for any organization, including a university setting; I refer to supervision. I know that the concept of supervision, as it has been developed in social work, is avoided in the university. Academic freedom is a condition so essential for achieving the objectives of university life that there has been a reluctance to use the term, let alone to explore whether, in fact, there is actual or potential infringement of academic freedom when appropriate supervision is provided. The rationale that I have heard is that the teacher must be free to teach the truth—or his compartment of the truth—as he sees it and is best left to his own devices in his endeavors. I think I would have been quick to detect any inhibition to my sense of freedom to perform with my students in the way most natural for me and most appropriate for my teaching purposes. I can therefore in clear conscience assert that whether it is called supervision, or mentorship, or consultation, we have here a useful administrative structure. If it is used appropriately, it provides time for the inductee to meet regularly once a week during his first year at a new school with a senior professor for thinking through the objectives of a course, familiarizing himself with approaches used by the school in the achieving of these objectives, testing his own ideas, receiving support and confirmation of his efforts—in short, using one of the most precious and richest resources in the school setting, the faculty. The availability and use of this source of helpfulness is not only stimulating and challenging but it also releases creative energy.

I received such supervision from the appropriate individuals for each of my course assignments in my original teaching area as well as my new ones. It was highly individualized in each instance, and must have been exceedingly skillful because it felt helpful and reassuring, never burdensome. Let us note, however, that administratively it is burdensome, for it imposes on the several senior professors a responsibility that may be overlooked in the listing of teaching load. I should note also that the special arrangement and relationships I have just described supplement a regular procedure wherein all the teachers of the same course meet periodically throughout each year to share ideas and coordinate assignments, bibliographies, and such matters as are appropriately coordinated, while leaving a maximum of opportunity for individuality and creativity.

Now for my final point—the "feeling" phase of induction. A faculty is an organism with a unique life of its own—its traditions, its common experience, its own communicative networks—in short, its own way of getting its tasks accomplished. Official membership in a faculty for a new professor is established arbitrarily by administrative fiat, but psychological membership must be worked at and earned. As a group worker I was, perhaps, especially interested in these dynamics. The new member—all of the verbal welcoming notwithstanding—is an outsider who does not share in the past life of this group —its lore and its way of working. He brings with him ties, not yet broken, with the group which he has left, and he is surprised by the nostalgia which is evoked. Comparisons are inevitable, even though there is no call for comparison. The new group cannot deny that it is wondering "how does he see us?," while at the same time affirming its pride in all of the patterns of thinking and operating which it has developed. The new member is, therefore, at first, primarily a learner. Before he can make his contribution, he must develop a perspective. He is, therefore, either a listener or an "information seeker" at faculty and committee meetings, and he must learn to be comfortable with these roles—quite different from what he had been doing only recently. Correspondingly, the in-group must acknowledge unto itself that as it incorporates new members into its body, it too will be changing. None will be the same as before. The anticipation of change is never easy, and living through change means hard work. There follows a fascinating period in which there are tentative feelers in both directions, a mutual testing of each other. This process takes time, it cannot be telescoped, and there are no short cuts. And almost imperceptibly, the predominant use of the pronoun "you" which marks the earlier stages is replaced by the pronoun "we." This changed feeling is the final stage of the induction process to which I referred earlier, wherein a status of belonging and mutuality is accomplished.

These dynamics are generally known and understood, yet we usually think of them in connection with groups we are observing or for whose productivity we have an assigned responsibility, less often when we are the central actors. I am suggesting that there are implications in these inevitable dynamics of value in planning for the induction of new members to a faculty. The new member must be given time to find his rightful place in a group which has a history of its own and one which is different from any other.

My thesis has been that the induction of a new faculty member is not something that takes care of itself. It is a process which should be planned. There are identifiable phases in the process which will be experienced, whatever the background of the inductee, but for each it will be highly individualized. Responsibility for this process is shared by the administration, faculty members, and the inductee. Out of the planning and shared responsibility can be realized the opportunity for human enrichment and professional revitalization.

Part III

"... And Gladly Teach"

"...AND GLADLY TEACH"

How much of teaching ability is an art which cannot be "learned," and how much of the ability to teach is both teachable and learnable is a question which will not be settled through rhetoric. Clarity and conviction will emerge with the accumulation of understanding about the teacher-learner transaction, an understanding whose frontier is constantly being expanded. For those who are convinced, the concept encompasses much more than mechanics or technical skills. It refers to an ability, based upon communicable philosophy, about the objectives of an educational activity, and a describable body of knowledge about how the learner learns, as well as knowledge and skill in communication, in the organization of curriculum, and the appropriate use of a range of methodologies.

It would be futile to attempt to collect in one place even representative selections from available resources in each of these areas for the strengthening of the "teaching component." Instead, two beautiful statements, each by a gifted "master teacher" have been selected. The manner in which they weave art and skill into harmonious support of each other will serve the purposes of this part of this volume. They place the good teacher—and good teaching—in a worthy light. They speak of the rewards of teaching and what it demands of one. They are frankly inspirational. Senior faculty will identify and reaffirm their calling. New faculty will find their decision to teach strengthened and in their desire to become "good teachers" they will be encouraged.

THE REQUIREMENTS AND REWARDS
FOR TEACHING

by Ruth E. Smalley*

It has often been said that social work is both a science and an art. Can it be both? And if it can be, and is, what kind of question, problem, dilemma does that pose for social work education, for teachers, for the finding and preparing of new teachers, for practitioners asking themselves whether they want to be, and can become teachers of social work? For a definition of terms, we consult the lexicon:

> *Science:* Knowledge as of facts, phenomena laws, and proximate causes gained and verified by exact observation, organized experiment, and correct thinking; an exact systematic statement or classification of knowledge concerning some subject or group of subjects.

> *Art:* Skill in performance; that which is produced by skill and taste; inventive power; capacity for perfection in execution. The skillful systematic arrangement or adaptation of means for the attainment of some end, especially by human endeavor as opposed to natural forces. And then this interesting bit: Knowledge may be a medley of facts which gain real value only when coordinated and systematized by the man of science. *Art* relates to something to be done or produced by skill; *science* to something to be known.

Since social workers must both know and be able to do, shall we, in any given school or department, employ some teachers who are scientists and some who are artists, and so come to a whole of education for a profession that asks its practitioners to be both? Will the result be students who take from whole scientists and whole artists and become themselves half and halves? Or will each student identify with the teacher most like his essential self and come out primarily scientist or primarily artist? Does social work need some scientists and some artists, or a blend of both, in all of its practitioners?

In other words, I am taking the position that every teacher in a school of social work is party to an operation that, taken as a whole, is preparing stu-

---

* Paper presented at the National Conference on Social Welfare, June 2, 1966, in Chicago, Illinois. Dr. Smalley retired that month as dean of the School of Social Work, University of Pennsylvania.

dents to do something, and that something is social work. In that sense, social work must be considered as an art, requiring skill for its execution, and making use of scientific and other forms of knowledge to achieve its ends.

I am making a further assumption, and that is that the practice of social work in any of its methods, and in any of its fields of practice, asks that its practitioners possess both knowledge and a very special kind of skill for putting knowledge to work for social work ends. The essential characteristic that distinguishes skill in social work method is that it is designed to free, to release power in individuals, groups, communities, or organizations, for their creative realization of themselves in ways which conduce to the common good.

Social work operates from certain values, and two seem to me to be primary: respect for the worth and dignity of every man, and concern that he have full opportunity to realize his potential. It also operates toward certain ends or purposes: to help society "work" for individuals, groups, and communities; to help individuals, groups, and communities become responsible contributive parts of society to the extent of their capabilities. The essence of the generic in all social work method is the practitioner's use of himself in a human relationship process to engage others—individuals, groups, communities, organizations—in working toward social ends. If we can agree on the nature of the profession and what it asks of its practitioners, we have a base for asking what it takes to be a teacher of social workers, and what the rewards of such teaching may be.

In addition to the art-science dilemma for social work, as social work educators we have the related certainty-doubt dilemma which has bearing on what is involved in teaching social work. The broad aims of a university are to transmit knowledge about man, his world, and his creations, but most of all to stimulate curiosity to encourage the pursuit of knowledge for the sake of knowledge, to encourage doubt and question, and to produce the skills, habits, and discipline necessary to work on questions and enlarge knowledge. A professional school of a university, and certainly a school of social work, seeks to produce students who are both questioning and sure—sure enough to act in the immediacy of the moment to accomplish ends with which the profession is charged by society to achieve, yet questioning and doubting enough of the very bases of their practice, the programs within which they work and the skill they employ, that they can participate in finding new and better ways to get the job done, in an ever-changing society.

So the practitioner who is considering becoming a teacher of social work is entering a field of education that asks him to help students become both doers and doubters, equipped with knowledge and skill for both activities; scientists, in the sense of being motivated, disciplined seekers of the knowledge necessary for their practice and their profession's practice; and artists in the sense of being creative in their use of themselves in relationship with others to free and release human power for social good, and social power for individual good. This holds, I submit, whatever the level of the educational operation.

Various relatively superficial reasons may attract some young practitioners to teaching: the alleged "status" of the "professor"; the wish or need to be an "authority" in relation to those who know less. But what attracts most, and what will keep each teacher there, and make him a good teacher, is the opportunity teaching offers him to arrive at the fullest possible self-realization. It isn't the answer for everyone. Some social workers prefer to, and should, continue in direct practice. To the direct service practitioner, or to the social actionist, teaching can be a frustration and an irritation, and should they come into the field of education for social work, that fact may be reflected in their teaching.

And now it is time to look more closely at what it is that great teaching asks in any field and what it yields to those who choose it as a way of life. I am turning to an old friend, a teacher of artists—Robert Henri—who spoke to his students as he walked among them while they worked, and who wrote *The Art Spirit* from jottings and notes made on those occasions. Some times he spoke of teaching: "A teacher should be an encourager."[1] This is a basic attitude which flows out from the teacher to the student and which evokes learning. The teacher catches the eye that has a sudden question, and, by his response, helps an uncertain student find the courage to speak. The teacher whose basic attitude is to be critical, to show off his knowledge or himself, or to show up a student's relative lack of knowledge, will not free the individual student or the class for learning, nor ever find for himself the deepest reward that teaching can hold. It is the warm sun that leads to the opening of the petals and it is the warm encouraging personality that leads to the flowering of the student. And again: "No knowledge is so easily found as when it is needed. Teachers have too long stood in the way and have said 'Go slowly. You want to be an artist before you have learned to draw.' Oh those long and dreary years of learning to draw. How can a student, after the drudgery, yet look at a man or an antique statue with any other emotion than a plumb-bob estimate of how many lengths of head he has."[2]

Here is something for the social work teacher. Imparting scientific knowledge about man, before the human encounter, or unrelated to the human encounter, can lead to an attitude of detached study and assessment and dull the capacity for appreciative helping engagement, so essential for the accomplishment of the task. And again: "Your work is intensely interesting to me. I come always to class with expectancy."[3]

It is that capacity to feel genuine and intense interest in the work of an-

[1] Robert Henri, *The Art Spirit* (Philadelphia: J. B. Lippincott, 1930), p. 78.
[2] *Ibid.*, p. 75.
[3] *Ibid.*, p. 153.

other, in the work of a student, to expect, which characterizes the great teacher, which calls forth the student's valuing of himself, his production, his work, and which stimulates his desire to improve it—to be interesting in what he is saying or doing or writing. As was earlier suggested, not everyone can feel this kind of primary interest in the work or the learning of another. Teaching is not for them.

Said Henri, "When the teacher is continually author, both of the question and its answer, it is not likely the answer will sink deep and get into service, as it will if the question is asked by the [student]."[4] How can the question be provoked, how can the thirst be developed that will prompt drinking from the Illyrian spring?

And again: "All this is to urge you to investigate, to read, to think. You will understand what the word 'techniques' refers to. You will wake up to the fact that the only education that counts is self education. There are the facilities of the school, its advices, there are books, strengths and weaknesses of those about you. All these things are good materials to the one who will use them constructively."[5] The great teacher knows it must be that way. The learning will be the student's own. The teacher is not just *constrained*, he is interested, he is fulfilled through putting himself, his knowledge, his experience *at the service* of his students. He is responsible in preparing materials, organizing and presenting materials, giving assignments, responding to what the student does and says, but he knows that central in the student's learning is the student himself. He will learn or he won't. For that the student must take final responsibility, and the teacher must let him take it, indeed help him to take it.

It is what the teacher is in himself, as a person, that the students will catch and use, each in his own way, and according to his own capacities. Meanness of spirit, shallowness, cynicism in a teacher of social work, whatever his "area," make it hard for students to use him to catch fire, to be fired by the great purposes of the profession, and to extend themselves to realize *their* best, in order that the profession may realize *its* best.

I have omitted many important requirements of the teacher, such as the necessities of pursuing, with vigor and enthusiasm, knowledge in his own teaching areas and related areas; and of contributing to the development of new knowledge, making thoughtful and painstaking preparation for each class session with recognition of its place in the time form, the rhythm of the school year; responding to student production not only in the course of classes, but through written comments on student papers; knowing and holding to standards of achievement which must be met for the student's progression to the next step—a difficult part of the teacher's responsibility, for it can

---

4 *Ibid.,* p. 170.

5 *Ibid.,* p. 215.

feel so counter to his nourishing and helping function, yet it can be integral to the helping, as well as essential out of accountability to school and profession; demonstrating interest in learning and using new methods and techniques of teaching as they give promise of more full accomplishment of teaching purpose. The specifics and techniques of method are not unimportant; they are of great importance. I seek merely to place them within the context of the essential nature of teaching, and what it asks of a particular kind of use of the teacher's self.

Just as the social work practitioner must find his own unique way of being a social work helper, within the values, purposes, and discipline of the profession, so too the new teacher must find his own way of being a social work teacher, whatever the level of the educational operation. Imagination, resourcefulness, and experimentation are required for devising ways of helping new teachers *become* teachers in the fullest sense, through a vigorous use of their highly individual selves, yet within the discipline of the profession for which they are preparing students, and the program within which they are teaching.

Frederick Allen's penetrating analysis of the "dilemma of growth" comes to mind here. He identifies the growth of a child as presenting a dilemma for parent and child, but his thesis has clear application for the induction of new teachers. He writes: "The dilemma for the mother can be formulated in this way: How can she direct and guide the life she has created toward a personally and socially acceptable goal, and yet allow the emergence of a separate and different self? How can she give all that she must without engulfing the child and making him no more than the product of her own will, for whom she could continue to feel full responsibility? How can she encourage creativeness in the product of her creation?"[6] About the growth dilemma for the child he writes: "How does he acquire the courage to be a self, different and separate from the self that created him?"[7]

A senior teacher to whom a new teacher may be assigned has the task of making herself, her experience, her knowledge, and her skill available to him without turning him into a carbon copy of herself. On the contrary, she should help and encourage him to be the kind of teacher that is an expression of his (desirably) highly individual self, bearing in mind the purposes of the educational program, and the contribution of others toward the attainment of the common goal.

The new teacher has the task of drawing on the wisdom, experience, and help of his mentor—but integrating what he learns into the different self that he is, as he learns to use that self as a teacher, and a teacher of social work.

---

[6] Frederick Allen, *Positive Aspects of Child Psychiatry* (New York: W. W. Norton, 1963).

[7] *Ibid.*, pp. 63-64.

So much more than "learning the ropes" is involved, although that is part of it. The task is to become *psychologically* a teacher, with all that that asks and offers.

But the prospective social work teacher has a responsibility too, one we should not and cannot take away from him. He may have to resist our efforts and blandishments to recruit him for teaching, unless teaching is right for him. His is the responsibility for looking beneath any surface reasons which may have attracted him to teaching initially (and beyond our importuning) as he asks himself whether he can truly find his best fulfillment through being the kind of teacher social work needs. Some of this he can discover only as he tries, with the planned devoted help of the individual school to which he comes. He will know with a deep certainty, despite all the inevitable ups and downs along the way, whether it is worth it to him to undergo the discipline of continuous study and independent professional production in writing and research, to sustain the steady and warm giving response to group after group of students whose resistances and negative fights are essential to their forward thrusts.

If he is really a teacher, he will give it up for no other calling on earth, for he will leave each class weary, certainly—but touched with new life too, having been a part, a central part, of another's becoming, many others becoming, not only social workers, surer of purpose and possessed of increased knowledge and skill for pursuing it, but *persons* of greater dimension.

". . . AND GLADLY TEACH"

by Helen Harris Perlman*

The thought of moral virtue filled his speech
And he would gladly learn and gladly teach.

CHAUCER

While still mourning the death of Charlotte Towle and remembering our long years of association in which I knew her as colleague, as friend, and as great teacher, I came to ponder that perennial question: What is a great teacher? What is he made up of? What attributes, what modes of relationship and communication, lift him to a special place in the minds and hearts of those who learned from him? Is there any point, I asked myself, in talking about it at all, in trying to analyze the practice of teaching past the point of paying tribute to those few who, like Charlotte Towle, lighted up the sky for some of the fortunate among us?

The probability is that great teachers are born, or shaped in childhood. There is a charisma about them, a giftedness that is grounded in some secure sense of self. There is some generosity of mind that is the result of an inner life so abundant and rich that it spills over to give its content to others. There is some free and open receptivity to encounters with new knowledge or ideas or people that makes them able to take them in with interest and delight. And there is their obvious pleasure in the exercise of mind and action that continuously shapes their subject matter to the needs of the students they teach. These qualities are gifts of person and are not to be had for the wishing; nor by self-command. We cannot wake up in the morning and say, "Today I simply must be creative"; nor can we adjure a fellow faculty member to "go develop a sense of humor" or "be ingenious."

One remembers the attributes of great teachers as they have been recounted by their admiring or loving former students, and remembers also that those accounts that go into published essays on teaching are, by this mark, already the accounts by gifted or at least highly literate students. I

* Paper presented at Plenary Session of the CSWE Fifteenth Annual Program Meeting, January 26, 1967, in Salt Lake City, Utah, and originally published in Journal of Education for Social Work, Vol. 3, No. 1 (Spring, 1967), pp. 41-51. Mrs. Perlman is on the faculty of the School of Social Service Administration, University of Chicago.

sometimes wonder how the run-of-the-mill student perceived Socrates or Mark Hopkins or those fabled Oxford dons who regularly tore their students to ribbons and thus, so the stories suggest, produced masters of logic and literary form. One reads descriptions of great teachers—Barzun, Highet, Edman—and others write to them, and at the moment of vicarious identification, one gets some heady sense that "I too have some part of this." Then the book is closed, the class hour approaches, there are butterflies in the stomach, yesterday's carefully developed notes look deadly, and one thinks, " 'and gladly teach!' But *how?*"

The problem for a teacher who would gladly teach so that his students might gladly learn is this: How can he become a good teacher by the exercise of his conscious intentions? Indeed this is the problem for schools of social work today. New schools and departments of social work are springing up everywhere overnight. They arise, not because the profession stands in full readiness to transmit its developed body of knowledge, but rather in response to a clamor for social work practitioners. The scramble for teachers results in faculties that, depending on one's point of view, may be called richly diverse or oddly assorted. In either case, the new recruit and the old hand both, in those lonely moments behind the closed office door, when they face only their teaching notes, ask themselves "How?"

Portraits of model teachers are posed and haloed. So rather than describing these, I ask myself what I believe is a basic question: "How do adults learn, anyhow?" Most educational theory stops short of adulthood. Yet students in schools of social work are adults, and even if we find that numbers of them are still involved in the identity and role confusions of adolescence or the natural work and love problems of early adulthood, it is still probable that their learning patterns are fairly well set and their capacities for changes are neither as flexible nor as plastic as they were before all those other teachers made their impress upon them. (Many of those other teachers, including parents, have done rather remarkable jobs, incidentally, in stretching and exercising growing minds and in supporting confidence in self-and-other.) But, even for the good learner, the tasks of professional education—and particularly social work education because of the many psychological hazards in social work itself—demand and challenge the young adult to a new kind of learning. It is not just that he learn more about this, that, or the other; he is equipped to do this as his transcripts confirm. It is that he must winnow, rearrange, and reorder everything he has already learned, plus what he is about to learn, into new configurations, shaped by questions of "So what is its use for social work? What does it say for what I or others ought to be and do?" Moreover, he must, at once, risk himself in using his barely grasped knowledge and know-how in the interest of others, and in this uncertain endeavor he will be subject to continuous scrutiny and evaluation. So his teachers, both in class and in field, face the task of changing the perspectives

111

and affects and behaviors of all but grown students with all but settled learning patterns.

Recently, several perspectives on the dynamics of personal change have emerged that bear upon learning and teaching of adults. Among them are the crisis and stress studies which show that at crucial points in an adult's life he is most vulnerable to, or accessible to, influence from "powerful others." "Crucialness" is inherent in the risks and shifts and investments of self that both career choice and the impact of field work force upon the social work student. "Powerful others" are those persons who are assumed to possess the means by which one's gratifications or goals can be achieved and who, further, proffer (or withhold) the nurture of love, safety, and recognition along the way. A number of recent inquiries into the core dynamics of socialization of learning in children point to the basic essential: a relationship that combines potency and affectivity, power and love. We are concerned with learning in adults, it is true, but it seems probable that here, too, though in diminished degree, *power and love, within a context of crucialness, are the dynamics of both unconscious changes and changes by conscious effort in our students.*[1]

Power and love are vested in—or are perceived by the student to be vested in—the role of teacher. The intensity with and degree to which these attributes are felt or sought in the teacher will depend, of course, on how much the student wants what the teacher has. One further conceptual perspective, derived from ego psychology and put forward notably by Robert White, adds to our view of teaching and learning. That is the concept of an innate drive for competence, which suggests that motivation in the human being consists not only of finding means to relieve tension and to achieve surcease of anxieties, but that it includes an insistent urge toward mastery and toward experiencing the self as effective and competent. When the teacher believes this to be true (not, one hopes, because of its oracular source, but because it confirms what he already has observed), he will take a certain position or view of the student that will affect his teaching content and relationships.

These several ideas—of power, of love, and of competence-motivation at a time of crucialness—are significant for the teacher of adults and for what he must do and be.

ON POWER

What is the nature of the power that students perceive and seek or sometimes fear in a teacher? The power that is feared is easy to identify; it stems

---

[1] In a recently published essay, "Socialization Through the Life Cycle," Orville Brim writes, "It appears that if society is to undertake basic re-socialization of adults in respect to motive and values it might well institutionalize in some form the high power and affectivity relationship characteristic of childhood learning." Orville G. Brim, Jr. and Stanton Wheeler, *Socialization After Childhood* (New York: John Wiley & Sons, 1966).

from the teacher's having the right and responsibility to assess the student as a learner. This has heightened meaning in a professional school because such assessment may shape the career goals of the student and affect his future. So grades and evaluations are touchy things in a professional school despite the graduate student's having learned to say that he knows grades don't really matter. But this evaluative power is not what infuses the student-teacher relationship with its major significance.

The power that is held by one who is to be an influential teacher is that of knowledge and know-how. The teacher must be seen to possess knowledge of the subject matter he teaches—possess it in the sense that he has not simply boned up on it, studied and crammed it, but that he has made it his own. He has come to possess it by mulling it over, having given the time and thought to view it in several perspectives. To use a physical analogy, he has incorporated his knowledge by long and careful tasting and smelling and chewing of it, and by "listening" to the tastes and textures of this food for thought before he has swallowed and digested it. He has made it his own by connecting it with what he already knew and believed, by a continuous process of mental shuttling between the special subject matter of his field, and between this and its import and uses in the profession, and between these and their relation to man in his daily life. His knowledge, then, is not a rigidified body of relevant facts and theories that spills forth on call like a tape from a computer machine; it is, rather, ordered, shaped, selected, lighted up, colored, and infused by the workover it is continuously undergoing in his mental and affective processes and in his interpretations of life experience. He becomes a *person* full of knowledge, not simply what we call "a brain." A "knowing" teacher knows his subject mentally and feelingly. He knows it not "by heart" but "*in* the heart." He warms it and warms to it continuously by his exercise and play with it and by his caring about whether it is well put together; he tends to its gaps and thin spots and tries to weave it whole. This kind of work to attain and expand knowledge is akin to loving.

In the academic situation, the teacher is held to have power when he "knows his stuff." His power of influence widens when he can show his students how to know theirs, how to grasp what they reach for. In the professional school, a further consideration marks the teacher of influence. It is that knowledge must be actually *demonstrated* to have power—that is, that it must have quick and apparent relevance and application to the learner's aim, which is to put knowing into action. In the professional school, then, the teacher's power must include not only knowledge but know-how. The student of social work must experience his teacher as someone who could, on call, apply the principles of interviewing he is teaching, construct and conduct a research project in an area of obfuscation, advise or testify before a legislative committee on social policy. Nowhere more than in a school of social work must there be the evidence to refute that dusty canard that he who knows

113

does and he who knows not *teaches*. That must first have been uttered by a cynical school dropout or a faculty member frustrated in a struggle for rank. But its persistence stands as a reminder to us all that, to seem powerful to the student, the teacher must show his know-how as well as his knowing. One reason for the field teacher's influence being exerted more potently than the classroom teacher's lies in the student's imputation to him of greater know-how. One problem for the teacher who has no direct social work experience is that there is often evident some missing trackage between his knowledge and its application.

I think back now to Charlotte Towle as a powerful teacher. She was a little woman; physically she always had to look up to her students. She was modest and unassuming in her bearing and manner. Fired by conviction and pushed by strong belief, she would speak out loud and clear and without compromise. But there were other times when she was uncertain or weary or tentative or simply self-contained. Yet I do not believe there was a single person among Charlotte Towle's students or colleagues who did not experience her as a major influence upon them. Wherein did her power lie? It lay in her knowledge and her know-how.

One could not be with Charlotte Towle for an hour without recognizing what a store of knowledge she possessed about the individual personality and the human condition, about all the living transactions between man and his social environment. She did not just "know" these things in a static way; what she knew was constantly at play in her, lighted up, now in one area now in another, by a continuous lively intelligence and probing curiosity. It was constantly being added to—not in some monolithic accretion, but in sifted, reshuffled, reorganized, and newly connected ways—by her continuous study combined with wide and varied nonprofessional reading, and by her insightful taking in of every new person and situation she encountered. Continuously she wove, unravelled, and rewove her ideas and observations and learnings so that the fabric of her knowledge was elastic and always in growth and change. You knew, when you opened some subject with her, that you were in the presence of a person who *possessed* what she had learned. Because she had made it her own, she felt comfortable with it, with neither the need to display it nor to feel uneasy when she was faced with a gap. When she said "I don't know," it carried neither embarrassment nor annoyance, but rather some pleased sense that there was something new that deserved exploration.

Charlotte Towle also had know-how. One sensed this not simply because she could explain principles of treatment in the classroom or because she had been highly regarded as a practitioner; one knew it with immediacy and validity in the encounters with her as teacher, consultant, colleague. She knew how to draw out and to feed into a person's own potentials and strengths, how to free initiative in others, how to empathize and support, how to differ without rancor or threat, and how to criticize without either

114

hedging or attacking. She had the know-how, in short, to deal with another person in ways that undergirded him at the same time as he was being influenced to change. She demonstrated this in her everyday contacts with students and colleagues.

Some of this power of knowledge and know-how was, of course, inherent and unique to the person of Charlotte Towle. But much of it was worked at by her, cultivated over the years of self-disciplined open-mindedness and responsibility. It is this combination of self-discipline, open-mindedness, and scholarly responsibility that I believe can be emulated and learned, by those who aspire to be potent teachers. It does not matter that one may never match one's model. What does matter is that the essential attributes of the model are understood and may serve as a constant inner touchstone against which to test and change one's own operations as a learner-teacher.

ON LOVE

To be potent in changing the minds and behaviors of adults, there must combine with knowledge and know-how the power of love. In what sense does a teacher love and show love? At the least, and fundamentally, he must love his subject matter. That is to say he must care about it; he must feel strongly that it is important, or that it matters, or that it has value. He must pour himself into it in some "heart-felt" ways. He must enjoy the pleasure of its company, of playing with it and examining it from all perspectives. He must see its faults and lameness. But, like the parent who pensively views his less-than-perfect child and forgives him for his imperfections and affirms his becoming more and better than he is, the teacher who loves his subject matter must be able to admit to and deplore its imperfections while at the same time affirm and defend its present and potential values.

A teacher's loving investment in his subject matter is a contagious thing. I suppose love is always contagious, warming to the people who come near to it, even though they may not be its direct recipients. All of us remember with warmth some teacher who affected us in benign ways, not because he was a brilliant theorist or a charismatic teacher, but because he was so obviously in love with what he taught. And all of us remember with distaste the hack who found no further delight or interest in his subject matter and served it up dead cold.

There is a second aspect of loving that infuses influential teaching: love of the learner. The teacher who loves his student does so in ways appropriate to this particular role relationship. It begins with receptivity to the person and the intent of the learner. It moves forward with the acceptance of his ambivalences (because all new learning tasks excite some "no" as well as "yes"), his doubts, his knowledge deficits. This acceptance is not total. It must combine with the expectation, held firm and clear, that the learner has the moti-

115

vation and the capacity to grapple with subject and self. Loving involves affirmation of the person and his potentials. It involves feeding in to him generously, with attention to his capacity for intake and with willingness on the part of the loving teacher to invent ways to engage him. But in the teaching role there can be no lowering of expectations and standards because both teacher and student are, by their implicit contract, engaged in an unalterable pursuit: the development of the student as a representative of a profession. When a teacher invests love in both the subject matter and the learner, his constant endeavor is to bring them happily together.

Having said this much about warming and freeing the student with love, I recall again all the stories of tutorial systems in English universities, which contradict my claims. They recount one-to-one sessions between teacher and student, consisting time after time of a ruthless tearing apart of the student's efforts, an often sadistic criticism, a wracking attack. And out of these experiences came some of the most brilliant, effective, clear-thinking philosophers, writers, and statesmen of our times. How so? What of love? One answer lies, I think, in recognizing that we have the testimonies of the survivors of that system; those who went down under it do not boast of it or commit it to print. A second explanation may be that those who went into this system and survived it went in already strong, fortified by mastery of all the stressful experiences that abound in an educational system that was set up to discipline and train an elite. They already felt power within themselves, and their sense of union and identification with their tutors derived from the devotion of both to the subject matter and the student's ambition to claim it for his own.

Students of social work are not typically formed of such stern stuff. Moreover, their subject matters, while often less intellectually rigorous, are more experientially demanding. For these reasons alone, the social work teacher's power of knowledge must be warmed by his reception of the learner as competent (until proved otherwise), as being appreciated for all his own unique qualities of mind and style, and as warranting respect for his intent and efforts, if not always for their outcomes. Criticism there must be, but it should be accompanied by guidance for change (or decision that change is not possible) and by concern for the learner's own integrity.

When I speak of the teacher's love of the learner I do not for a moment mean that engulfing, dependency-creating overseeing of every sentence the student speaks, or that anxious rehearsal of every move he is to make. I speak rather of that interest in the individual student, in receiving him as someone who has a style of his own, a potential for shaping it and not abandoning it to the principles of his profession, and as a person who must risk himself and therefore who will be expected to make some mistakes, and who must be allowed to be foolish at times.

The influence of Charlotte Towle through the several kinds of loving spoken of made its deep impress on those who learned from her. She poured

116

herself unstintingly into her several subject matters. Her class preparation, her consideration of how to meet student need, how to select, shape, and phrase her knowledge so that it would be meaningful and retained for use by the learner—these considerations were her central concerns. Sometimes she was surprised at some particularly happy turn of concept or phrase she invented and she shared with her students her frank delight at having found some new connections or some new way of imparting knowledge. Her devoted commitment and pleasure in what she taught was open and a delight to witness.

She loved learners as she loved learning. I have never known anyone who continuously gave so much of her time, energy, and thinking to helping others with their learning tasks. Her comments on student papers were running dialogues with them, praising or taking issue as the case might be, never simply marking right or wrong, good or poor, yes or no, but spelling out the issue that was overlooked, supplementing the undeveloped idea, pointing out the alternatives. She took delight in all growing things and their nurture, and her students and those others of us who learned from her were among them.

Can loving be imitated and learned? Can a person who undertakes to teach set his jaw and determine that he is going to love his subject matter and his students and then go and do so? Perhaps; but only to a limited degree. Certainly there are days for each of us when the appearance of another book on our special subject matter makes us recoil in self-defense, protesting that we don't want to know one more thing about penguins or people or processes. There are days when each of us thinks that a university would be a marvelous place to work if only there were no students in it. But these days are few and far between and, if they are not, they are the surest signal to the teacher to find his niche elsewhere. Perhaps this negative criterion is the most that one can say about the loving aspects of teaching. One cannot command loving either of knowledge or learners. One can only say quite surely that if there is not a fairly continuous sense that what one teaches is vital and important and even beautiful in some ways, and if, from this, there is not some wish and urge to share the pleasure of this matter with others and to bring others to want it, then as a teacher, one will have very little influence upon students. Perhaps in the hiring of prospective teachers, deans should ask not just "what do you know?" but "how do you *feel* about what you know and about putting yourself out to bring others—the sometimes reluctant or skeptical or ambivalent students—to want to involve themselves in learning?"

ON COMPETENCE

The teacher's powers of knowledge and its uses and his demonstrated investment both in the learner and the field of endeavor are, then, two major forces in transforming the student into a professional person. The third force

117

drives within the student himself. But it needs the teacher's recognition, support, and stimulation to find its fullest and most appropriate expression. I speak now of the drive for effectance, the motivation inherent in each of us to strive for mastery, self-actualization, competence.

These different terms—effectance, mastery, self-actualization, competence—have been put forward in recent years by various ego psychologists (Hendrick, Maslow, and White among others) to name a phenomenon that earlier psychodynamic theory had left underdeveloped. It is the phenomenon of an innate motive beyond what is explained by the concepts of libidinal and aggressive drives: the drive for pleasure that is experienced in the exercise of the ego—of its powers of muscle and mind—in the pursuit of higher and still higher levels of effectiveness and sense of competence.

The concept of the innate drive for competence as present and developing in the autonomous ego (rather than as some neutralization and sublimation of more primitive instincts) is a concept that seems particularly useful in the educational situation. In essence, it affirms that our students, selected by us because they have proved their capacity to learn, carry within them strong thrusts to explore their world beyond what they have done thus far, to learn more and better and for an avowed purpose, and to use their minds and complete selves either for the pleasure it gives them now or for the promise of pleasurable competence ahead or both. There are exceptions to be sure. There are those among our students in whom capacity turns out not to match drive and those in whom the competence drive has been checked or warped by long-standing emotional barriers. Not all graduate students are free to pour their energies into learning if only we give them the chance. But, conservatively speaking, it seems that if a teacher finds the idea of competence-motivation compatible with his own observations and experience, it may serve as a useful stance or viewing point for his relationship to the learner and that of the learner to the subject matter.

This viewing stance promises some fresh perspectives on teaching and learning. The idea of a competence drive shifts the focus of teacher attention from the student's dependency needs to his coping capacity. It focuses less on his expectable inadequacies in a new situation and more upon undergirding his potential, waiting-to-be-tried competences. It suggests that the one-to-one tutorial relationship of field work with its frequent overprotectiveness may not be as essential as we once thought it to be when we conceived of the student as necessarily dependent and needful. It suggests that classroom teachers might well raise their expectation levels and expand opportunities for the students' greater freedom of inquiry and greater exercise of originality. Perhaps we have not recognized or treasured enough the driving initiative and ideals and the impatient push for action with which so many of our young students enter our schools today. Perhaps we have not been ingenious enough in modifying our instructional methods or curriculum arrangements

118

to match and make the most of the students' robust, even though brash, drive to become and to do better as quickly as possible.

How fully and pleasurably a student experiences the exercise of his powers of thought and action depends heavily upon his teachers. The opportunity he is afforded to take risks; the support he gets for using his initiative; the respectful consideration he gets for his ideas, far out though they may be, not in uncritical acceptance of them but in acceptance of his intentions while his notions are subjected to the light of greater knowledge or cooler reason; the expectation that he is capable and competent as a learner until he proves otherwise; the freedom he is given to try himself provided that he is within the boundaries of his professional role and purpose—all these opportunities may be opened to the student by the teacher who views him as a learner striving for actualization as a professional person.

Charlotte Towle knew this intuitively. In her usual disciplined way, she lifted her bone-and-marrow knowledge to her conscious consideration. When ego psychologists were only beginning to put forward their propositions about the autonomous ego and its conflict-free functions, Charlotte Towle had already written, "There is evidence in human behavior that, in contrast to the tendency towards resistence to change and regression to the past, there is also a strong and inevitable impulse toward progression . . . the human personality in the process of maturing begins to reach out beyond itself."[2] She believed this, and until some learning or self-management problem showed itself she presumed her students to be motivated and able to work and reach beyond themselves. Before the perception and affect-changing powers of cognition were given full recognition by most psychologists or educators, Charlotte Towle had observed and articulated these powers. She wrote some years ago, "in an educational situation the means to the end of effecting change in feeling is through the intellect. New ideas, new intellectual orientation may bring a change in feeling, thinking, and action in the context of an influential relationship."[3] She did not for a moment forget the dynamic matrix of the supporting relationship that provides the learner's safety island. But she was also clear about the difference between an educational and a therapeutic focus and in the former she understood the many aspects of ego strength, including the cognitive, that empowered the learner. Her belief in the "impulse toward progression" combined with her love for the learner. Never was the learner her creature; he was seen, rather, as a self-motivated source of potential professional power. The dialogue between Charlotte Towle and a learner—whether that learner was a first-year student

---

[2] *Common Human Needs*, Public Assistance Report #8, 1945. In its most recent re-issue (NASW, 1965), this quotation will be found on p. 43.

[3] Charlotte Towle, "The Contribution of Education for Social Casework to Practice," *Social Casework*, October, 1950.

or a colleague—was a matter of respectfully shared knowledge, opinion, and judgment. If in the end you disagreed, there was no threat to her or to you. She took pleasure in seeing difference asserted and therefore left one free to be himself. This is probably the truest mark of the great teacher: that he gives generously of his knowledge and notions and attention to the student and then, having offered such nurture, he does no violence to the independence of the learner; he leaves him free to be himself. In some part it is caring for the individuality of the "other" that enables a teacher to leave his student free, and in some part it is belief in the learner's own drive for competence. Charlotte Towle combined this caring and belief.

To return now to the question posed at the outset, is there any point to studying the model of a great teacher? Is there any purpose in examining those forces and attributes that account for the quickening and illumination of communication between teacher and learner? After all, teachers, like students, must essentially be and act themselves. And teachers, usually older by some years than students, tend to be long-patterned in their ways of operating. But it is also true that teachers, like students, are moved and shaped by powerful and loving relationships and by their competence motivation.

The powerful "other" that moves the teacher is usually in the nature of a professional ego ideal. That ego ideal may be incorporated in the living person of an "other," a colleague, for instance, who demonstrates and stands for what one would like to be able to do and be. One can never replicate him but one can emulate him. One can observe what he does that is good, what seems useful, what is admirable, and what makes him effective, and, from his repertoire, it is possible to borrow those parts that fit into one's own and that promise to enhance one's powers. Or, the professional ego ideal may be shaped and colored by teachers in one's past, or even those only read about who, in their teaching role, acted in ways held to be admirable or potent. Through identification with them or the taking in of parts of them one's sense of strength and of responsibility as a teacher grows. When one looks closely at the great teachers, one sees not only their innate gifts of intellect and communion, but also their disciplined engagement with their subject matter and with its transmission. The "power" we impute to the great teacher is some combined mastery of an area of knowledge and mastery of self as its interpreter.

This is where love comes in. It must be there to warm the teacher's stretching powers. If he is to be an interpreter of the subject matter in which he has invested he must also invest himself in attentive reception and nurture of those who are to receive his interpretations. He will need to become a matchmaker, if you will, between his subject matter and his "object matter," the students.

To some degree love can be worked at. Indeed it must be—even that loving that leaps in us spontaneously as between a man and woman or parent and child. There are those moments or phases of a relationship where, because of transient rejection or indifference or antagonism, one must work at rearranging one's self, acting with patience though one may feel only irritation, acting the wish to understand though one may feel only anger, reaching out to receive the other though one may feel like slamming a door shut. All love must be worked at now and again. We do so when we feel that the effort will warm us and enhance the reciprocal relationship again. The behaviors of affect and actions that convey "love," or, if you prefer, "I like and value you," become infused with genuine feeling when they are rewarded by responsiveness.

When, through these efforts, the teacher achieves a happy engagement—when a student's eyes light up with new understanding, or he cries "aha!" or, less dramatically, he merely affirms by his respectful attention and dogged study that he has faith that this is good and useful—then the teacher gets his reward. He will find in himself some stir and change in his feeling toward the student or the student body that is embarrassingly close to love. We simply cannot help loving that upon which we have some benign influence, whether it is a homely, scraggly ivy plant on an office desk that finally puts forth a shoot because we have tended and watered it or a thorny student who suddenly lights up one day and becomes a learner. That small reward for the hard work that loving often requires is a powerful incentive for further effort on the teacher's part.

All of us, students and teachers alike, strive to be the cause of some "good" effects, the cause of some changes that are held to be desirable. This is what the concept of motivation for competence expresses. And this is what pushes us as teachers to stretch our sights and our efforts: to read, study, discuss, wonder; to turn the merciless light of question upon cherished beliefs to see if they are true or only comfortable; to shake up and blow the dust off old ideas to see if they are still relevant; to continuously answer the nagging questions of utility to professional responsibility and practice. This is what makes us want to lend ourselves to the student and then to support and stimulate him toward his own actualization as a member of our profession. This ideal of ourselves as being a "cause" in the development and change in a new generation, toward its achievement of what we hold to be good, is what drives us to develop and change ourselves, to invest ourselves in study and students toward our own greater competence. This is what sends us back year after year to ponder on teaching and, despite the grind and the groaning, to gladly teach.

BIBLIOGRAPHY

(The items that follow have been grouped into two categories: (1) The University, Graduate, and Professional Education; and (2) The Field of Social Work Education, with subcategories within both of these broad classes. No attempt has been made to present an exhaustive listing. The intent is to provide the reader who wishes to pursue one or another line of inquiry with points of entry into the vast literature available. Some items are included because they are sources of additional bibliography; a few broad overviews and some specific references are included primarily because they reflect and represent the scope of literature and the periodical resources. Ed.)

THE UNIVERSITY, GRADUATE, AND PROFESSIONAL EDUCATION

General Overview and Issues

Association for Higher Education. *Current Issues In Higher Education*, G. Kerry Smith, ed., 1959 and 1960. Washington, D.C.: National Education Association.

Barzun, Jacques. *Teacher in America*. Garden City, N.Y.: Doubleday & Co., 1954.

Becker, Howard S. and Carper, James W. "The Development of Identification with an Occupation," *American Journal of Sociology*, Vol. LXI, No. 4 (January, 1956), pp. 289-298.

Berelson, Bernard. *Graduate Education in the United States*. New York: McGraw-Hill, 1960.

Blauch, Lloyd E. "Professional Education," in *Encyclopedia of Educational Research*, Chester W. H. Harris, ed., for the American Educational Research Association. New York: Macmillan Co., 1960, pp. 1056-63.

Blessing, James H. *Graduate Education: An Annotated Bibliography*. Washington, D.C.: U.S. Government Printing Office, 1961.

Borrowman, Merle L., ed. *Teacher Education in America: A Documentary History*. New York: Teachers' College, Columbia University, 1965.

Carmichael, Oliver C. *Graduate Education*. New York: Harper & Row, 1961.

Conant, James B. *The Education of American Teachers*. New York: McGraw-Hill, 1963.

Diekhoff, John S. *The Domain of the Faculty*. New York: Harper & Row, 1956, pp. 55 ff.

Daedalus, Vol. 92, No. 4 (Fall, 1963), entire issue entitled *The Professions: U.S.A.*

Daedalus, Vol. 93, No. 4 (Fall, 1964), entire issue entitled *The Contemporary University: U.S.A.*

Frankel, Charles, ed. *Issues In University Education: Essays by Ten American Scholars.* New York: Harper & Row, 1959.

Higher Education for American Democracy: A Report of the President's Commission on Higher Education. Vol. 4. *Staffing Higher Education.* New York: Harper & Row, 1947.
See also critiques by Benjamin, Harold R. W., "Ph.D.'s Preferred," *Journal of Higher Education*, Vol. 19, No. 4 (April, 1948), pp. 189-193; and Jones, Charles W., "The Truman Report and the Graduate Schools," *Journal of Higher Education*, Vol. 20, No. 7 (October, 1949), pp. 355-359.

Ingham, R. J., ed. *Institutional Backgrounds of Adult Education.* Boston: Center for the Study of Liberal Education for Adults, 1966.

Mayhen, Lewis B. "The Literature of Higher Education," *Educational Record*, Vol. 46, No. 1 (Winter, 1965), pp. 5-32.

McGlothlin, William. *Patterns of Professional Education.* New York: G. P. Putnam's Sons, 1960.

————. "The Aims of Professional Education." *Education For Social Work: 1958 Proceedings of the Sixth Annual Program Meeting,* Council on Social Work Education, 1958, pp. 20-31.

————. *The Professional Schools.* New York: Center For Applied Research In Education, 1964.

McGrath, Earl J. "The Goals of Higher Education," *Journal of Higher Education*, Vol. 20, No. 4 (April, 1949), pp. 171-180.

National Society for the Study of Education. *Education For The Professions.* 61st Yearbook, Part II, Nelson B. Henry, ed. Chicago: National Society for the Study of Education, 1962.

Perkins, James A. *The University in Transition.* Princeton: Princeton University Press, 1966.

Riesman, David. "The Academic Career: Notes on Recruitment and Colleagueship," *Daedalus*, Vol. 88, No. 1 (Winter, 1959), pp. 147-169.

Sanford, Nevitt, ed. *The American College: A Psychological and Social Interpretation of Higher Learning.* New York: John Wiley and Sons, Inc., 1962. See Chapter VII, "Changing Functions of the College Professor," by Robert Knapp, pp. 290-311.

Walters, Everett, ed. *Graduate Education Today.* Washington, D.C.: American Council on Education, 1965.

Whitehead, Alfred North. *The Aims of Education.* New York: Macmillan, 1929.

Woodring, Paul, "The Profession of College Teaching," *Journal of Higher Education*, Vol. 31, No. 5 (May, 1960), pp. 280-282.

On the Doctorate

Bent, Henry E. "Professionalization of the Ph.D. Degree," *Journal of Higher Education*, Vol. 30, No. 3 (March, 1959), pp. 140-145.

Brogan, Albert P. "Restoring the Master's Degree," *Graduate Journal*, Vol. 1, No. 1 (Spring, 1958), pp. 34-40.

Dodd, Stuart C. "A Ph.D. Defined in Three Tenses," *Journal of Educational Sociology*, Vol. 30, No. 9 (May, 1957), pp. 423-427.

Hunt, Erling M. "An Ed.D. for College Teachers," *Journal of Teacher Education*, Vol. 13, No. 3 (September, 1962), pp. 279-283.

Ness, Frederic W. "The Case of the Lingering Degree," *Saturday Review*, January 15, 1966, pp. 64 ff.

Walters, Everett. "The Immutable Ph.D." *Saturday Review*, January 15, 1966, pp. 62 ff.

——————. "A New Degree for College Teachers," *Journal of Higher Education*, Vol. 31, No. 5 (May, 1960), pp. 282-284.

——————. "What Degree for College Teachers?" *Journal of Higher Education*, Vol. 31, No. 2 (February, 1960), pp. 69-74.

Wilson, O. Meredith. "The Ph.D. Program as Preparation for College Teaching," *Association of American Colleges Bulletin*, Vol. 44, No. 1 (March, 1958), pp. 55-59.

On Academic Freedom

Hofstadter, Richard and Metzger, Walter P. *The Development of Academic Freedom in the United States*. New York: Columbia University Press, 1955.

On The Improvement of Teaching

American Association of Colleges for Teacher Education. *Proceedings Eighteenth Yearbook (Action For Improvement of Teaching Education)*. Washington, D.C.: American Association of Colleges of Teacher Education, 1965.

Beach, Mark. "Promoting Good Teaching in the Microversity," *Journal of Higher Education*, Vol. 37, No. 6 (June, 1966), pp. 301-306.

Broudy, Harry. "The Education of Teachers," *Journal of Teacher Education*, Vol. 13, No. 3 (September, 1962), pp. 284-291.

Bruner, Jerome S. *The Process of Education*. Cambridge: Harvard University Press, 1960.

Cottrell, Donald B., ed. *Teacher Education For A Free People*. Oneonta, New York: The American Association of Colleges For Teacher Education, 1956.

Daedalus, Vol. 94, No. 3 (Summer, 1965), entire issue entitled *Creativity And Learning: U.S.A.*

Eckert, Ruth E. "Some Neglected Aspects In The Preparation of College Teachers," *Journal of General Education*, Vol. 3, No. 2 (January, 1949), pp. 137-144.

Estrin, Herman A. and Goode, Delmer M. *Improving College and University Teaching*. Dubuque, Iowa: W. C. Brown Co., 1964.

Fahey, George and Masoner, Paul. "An Interdisciplinary Seminar in College Teaching," *Journal of Teacher Education*, Vol. 11, No. 3 (September, 1960), pp. 391-397.

Gage, Norman L., ed. *Handbook of Research on Teaching*. Chicago: American Educational Research Association, Rand McNally, 1963.

Gardner, John W. *Excellence: Can We be Equal and Excellent Too?* New York: Harper & Row, 1961.

——————. *Self-Renewal: The Individual and the Innovative Society*. New York: Harper & Row, 1963.

Goheen, Robert F. "The Teacher in the University," *School and Society*, Vol. 94, No. 2276 (April 2, 1966), pp. 177-179.

Gusfield, Joseph and Riesman, David. "Faculty Culture and Academic Careers: Some Sources of Innovation in Higher Education," *Sociology of Education*, Vol. 37, No. 4 (Summer, 1964), pp. 281-305.

Hamachek, Don E., ed. *The Self in Growth, Teaching and Learning*. Englewood Cliffs, N.J.: Prentice Hall, 1965.

Henri, Robert. *The Art Spirit*. Philadelphia: J. B. Lippincott Co., 1930.

Lee, Calvin B. T., ed. *Improving College Teaching*. Washington: American Council on Education, 1967.

Little, J. Kenneth. "Graduate Education," in *Encyclopedia of Educational Research*, Chester W. H. Harris, ed., for the American Educational Research Association. New York: Macmillan Co., 1960, pp. 593-602.

McCutcheon, Roger P. "The Preparation of College Teachers," *Graduate Journal*, Vol. 1, No. 2 (Fall, 1958), pp. 139-143.

National Education Association of the United States. *Remaking the World of the Career Teacher*. Washington: National Education Association of the United States, 1966.

Pullias, Earl V. and Lockhart, Aileene et al. *Toward Excellence in College Teaching*. Dubuque, Iowa: W. C. Brown Co., 1963.

THE FIELD OF SOCIAL WORK EDUCATION

General Overview and Issues

Abbott, Edith. *Social Welfare and Professional Education*. Chicago: University of Chicago Press, 1931.

Blackey, Eileen. "Issues in Social Work Education—New and Changing Demands Made of the Profession," *Education For Social Work: 1964 Proceedings of the Twelfth Annual Program Meeting*, Council on Social Work Education, 1964, pp. 75-89.

Boehm, Werner W., ed. *Objectives of the Social Work Curriculum*. Vol. I of the Report of the Curriculum Study. New York: Council on Social Work Education, 1959.

Council on Social Work Education. *Social Work Education and Social Welfare Manpower: Present Realities and Future Imperatives*. New York: Council on Social Work Education, 1965.

——————. *Contemporary Education For Social Work In The United States*. New York: Council on Social Work Education, 1966.

—————. *Field Instruction In Graduate Social Work Education—Old Problems and New Proposals.* New York: Council on Social Work Education, 1966.

—————. *Statistics on Social Work Education, 1967,* Frank M. Loewenberg, ed. New York: Council on Social Work Education, 1967.

Gardner, John W. "Remarks," at the Fourteenth Annual Program Meeting of the Council on Social Work Education. *Journal of Social Work Education,* Vol. 2, No. 1 (Spring, 1966), pp. 5-9.

Hollis, Ernest W. and Taylor, Alice. *Social Work Education in the United States.* New York: Columbia University Press, 1951.

Jennings, Daniel. "Characteristics of Faculty Members at Graduate Professional Schools of Social Work in the United States and Canada" (Unpublished Doctoral Dissertation, Catholic University, 1965). See also paper based on this dissertation, "Characteristics of Social Work Faculty Members," *Social Work Education Reporter,* Vol. 14, No. 3 (September, 1966), pp. 23 ff.

Kadushin, Alfred. "Two Problems of the Graduate Program: Level and Content," *Journal of Education For Social Work,* Vol. 1, No. 1 (Spring, 1965), pp. 33-46.

Kendall, Katherine A. "Choices To Be Made in Social Work Education," in *Social Work Practice, 1966.* New York: National Conference on Social Welfare, 1966.

Kindelsperger, Walter L. "Responsible Entry into the Profession—Some Current Issues," *Journal of Education For Social Work,* Vol. 2, No. 1 (Spring, 1966), pp. 41-51.

Maxwell, Jean M. "New Settings For Field Instruction," *Social Work Education Reporter,* Vol. 14, No. 3 (September, 1966), pp. 30 ff.

Merle, Sherman. *Survey of Undergraduate Programs in Social Welfare: Programs, Faculty, Students.* New York: Council on Social Work Education, 1967.

National Association of Social Workers. *Encyclopedia of Social Work.* Harry L. Lurie, ed. New York: National Association of Social Workers, 1965. See "History of American Social Work," by John C. Kidneigh, pp. 3-19; "Education for Social Work," by Rachel B. Marks, pp. 277-283; and "Personnel in Social Work," by Mary R. Baker, pp. 532-540.

"Official Statement of Curriculum Policy For The Master's Degree Program in Graduate Professional Schools of Social Work," adopted by the Board of Directors of the Council on Social Work Education, October 19, 1962.

Onken, Richard. *Survey of Faculty in Graduate Schools of Social Work.* New York: Council on Social Work Education, 1968.

Stein, Herman D. "Cross Currents in Practice, Undergraduate and Graduate Education in Social Work," *Journal of Education for Social Work,* Vol. I, No. 1 (Spring, 1965), pp. 56-57.

United States Department of Health, Education, and Welfare. *Closing The Gap . . . In Social Work Manpower.* Report of the Departmental Task Force on Social Work Education and Manpower. Washington: U.S. Department of Health, Education, and Welfare, 1965.

ON THE PREPARATION OF SOCIAL WORK EDUCATORS

Connery, Maurice F. "Becoming A Social Work Educator," paper presented at the Thirteenth Annual Program Meeting, Council on Social Work Education, Denver, January, 1965.

Council on Social Work Education. "From Practitioner To Teacher," Institute Reports—1957 and 1958. (Unpublished).

Meier, Elizabeth G. "Preparation For Teaching Social Work," *Social Work Education Reporter*, Vol. 13, No. 3 (September, 1965), pp. 14 ff.

Pins, Arnulf M. *Who Chooses Social Work, When and Why?* New York: Council on Social Work Education, 1963.

—————. "A Proposed Curriculum With A Practice Emphasis In Doctoral Programs." *Social Work Education Reporter*, Vol. 14, No. 3 (September, 1966), pp. 33 ff.

Regensburg, Jeanette, ed. *Some Educational Patterns In Doctoral Programs In Schools of Social Work.* New York: Council on Social Work Education, 1966.

Soffen, Joseph. *Faculty Development in Professional Education.* New York: Council on Social Work Education, 1967.

Towle, Charlotte. "The Distinctive Attributes of Education For Social Work," *Social Work Journal*, Vol. 33, No. 2 (April, 1952), pp. 63 ff.

Tyler, Ralph W. "Distinctive Attributes of Education For The Professions," *Social Work Journal*, Vol. 33, No. 2 (April, 1952), pp. 55 ff.

On Teaching in Social Work

Two classics for social work teachers are:

Reynolds, Bertha Capen. *Learning and Teaching in the Practice of Social Work.* New York: Rinehart and Co., 1942.

Towle, Charlotte. *The Learner in Education for the Professions.* Chicago: University of Chicago Press, 1954.

The reader will find the *Publications Catalog* of the Council on Social Work Education a major resource for readings on teaching in social work, under headings such as: Curriculum, Social Work Methods, Teaching Materials, and Methodology. Reports on Faculty Day Meetings at CSWE Annual Program Meetings, workshop position papers and discussions, and project and committee reports are identified.

Additional major resources from CSWE publications are:

Education for Social Work. Proceedings of Annual Program Meetings of the CSWE, annually 1952-1964. See, for example, Marguerite V. Pohek, "Toward a Methodology of Teaching," 1964, pp. 149-161.

Journal of Education for Social Work, published twice a year.

Pohek, Marguerite V., ed. *The Teacher's Compendium*, 1963.

The Social Work Education Reporter, published quarterly to reflect developments in social work education. Includes articles on teaching and a regular section, "Teaching News-Notes." See, as examples: Victoria Olds, "Activities to Improve the Quality of Instruction at a School of Social Work," Vol. 14, No. 3 (September, 1966), pp. 37 ff; and Mary Louise Somers, "Toward the Improvement of Social Work Teaching Methods and Materials," Vol. 14, No. 4 (December, 1966), pp. 28 ff.

A Sourcebook of Readings on Teaching in Social Work, 1965.

SELECTED CSWE PUBLICATIONS
IN FACULTY DEVELOPMENT

FACULTY DEVELOPMENT IN PROFESSIONAL EDUCATION: PROBLEMS OF PROPOSALS FOR RECRUITMENT, PRE-SERVICE, INDUCTION, AND CONTINUING DEVELOPMENT IN SOCIAL WORK EDUCATION, edited by Joseph Soffen. 1967.   (#67-63-08) $5.00

A SURVEY OF FACULTY IN GRADUATE SCHOOLS OF SOCIAL WORK, Richard Onken. 1968.   (#68-330-1) $3.00

REPORT OF AN INSTITUTE FOR COLLEGE FACULTY ON TEACHING A SOCIAL WELFARE COURSE, edited by Charles C. Crider. 1966.   (#66-9-21) $3.00

A SOURCE BOOK OF READINGS ON TEACHING IN SOCIAL WORK: REPRINTS OF SELECTED ARTICLES. 1965.   (#65-58-3) $3.00

THE TEACHER'S COMPENDIUM, compiled and edited by Marguerite V. Pohek. 1963.   (#63-50-1) $2.00

AN ANNOTATED BIBLIOGRAPHY ON AUDIOVISUAL INSTRUCTION IN PROFESSIONAL EDUCATION, Ida Oswald. 1967.   (#66-101-1) $3.00

EDUCATION FOR SOCIAL WORK: READINGS IN SOCIAL WORK, Vol. IV, compiled by Eileen Younghusband.   (#68-650-14) $3.00

SURVEY OF UNDERGRADUATE PROGRAMS IN SOCIAL WELFARE: PROGRAMS, FACULTY, STUDENTS, Sherman Merle. 1967.   (#67-63-15) $4.00